LIQUID · AIR-CANADA · AIR-BRIDGE · AIRBALL · AIRMAIL · ... RUGEL · AMATEUR SIDE · A...
· AUDI · AUDITOR · A... · BACK DOOR · BACK OF THE ... · ... · BAFFI...
...E HAWKER · BALLO... · BANANA BALL · BAND... · BANK SHOT · ... QUI...
BELLY ...GER · BELLY SHO... ...LY SNAP · BELT (TO) · ...O (TO) · BIG DOG (LET THE ...G DOG ... · BI...
(TO) ...OOD (NO) · ...DRY · BLUEPRI... IT (T... ...B... ...LIE TEES) · BO... REK · BO... D...

...NE BRIDGE · CENTER CUT) CHAINSAW LIE · CHAINSAW C... · CHARITY BALL · CHEEKS (HITTING W...
...ER · CHOPITA · CHUBBY · CHUCK WAGON · CHUNK · CHUNKY TUNA · CLEARCUTTING · CLEATS · CL...
...ACKER · COMMERCIAL JOB · COMPANY BALLS · CONDO GOLF · CONNECT (TO) · COW PASTURE · CR...
...N PATROL · DEAD · DE... ...AT · DEUCE · DEW-SWEEPERS · DIALING 8 · DIMPLEHEAD · DIMPLE PIMPL...
...E · D... LE BUZZARD ...OUBLE DOG ... S · DOUBLE LAUREL · DOUBLE-...EAKER · DOUBLE-GOLFST...
· DR... ...IVE BY SHO...ING · DRIV... ...WEDGE · DSP · DUB · ...UCK HO... ...DUDE · DUFFER · DU...

...RISCO · FRITO-LAY · FROG EYES · FROG HAIR · FRONT (THE) · FROSTY · FROZEN ROPE · FUDGE FACTO...
· GIRAFFE · GIRLIE · GIVE GIVE · GIZ · GOAT · GOING TO SCHOOL · GOLDEN FERRET · GOLF PRINCES...
...AFT · GRASSCUTTER · GREEN STALKER · GREEN LIGHT LIE · GREENIE · GRETZKY · GRINDER · GRIP · G...
...H... ...UR · HALF A S...OWMAN · HALF-HITCH · HAND-MA... IE · HAND... ...DGE · HANGING LIE · HAI...
...IT...HERDING / H... RIES · HIT A BARN! · HIT A HO... · HIT AND R... · HITLER · HOCKEY STIC...
...HU... · HI...MER · H...NT (IN THE) · ICE RINK · JAB · JA... IT U... JAIL · J...M · J...MALIES · JAMO...

...GH · LINDA RONDSTADT · LINT · LIP OUT · LIPROXY · LIPSTICK · LIZ TAYLOR · LOAF · LOBSTER · LOOGI...
...OBBITT · LUMBER · LUMBERYARD · MAKEABLE · MALLARD · MARBLE · MARINE CORPS GOLF · MAR...
...EL · MICK JAGGER · MICKEY MOUSE · MILEAGE · MILITARY GOLF · MISSABLE · MOLE · MONKE...
· MRS. DOUBTFIRE · MURDER · MUFF · MU...LIGAN · MULL... · MURDERERS' ROW · NAIL IT (TO) · NAIL...
...O... ...Y (TO) · NUR... ...B · OCEA... ...NE · OLD EQUA... · OLDSMOBILE SCRAMBLE · O...BLE...
...AM... ANDERSON (S...CHING FOR ...ANCAKE · PAR-... OURSE · PBS · PFC · PEGB...
· PI... ...DOWN THE) · P... NIB... NIBLIC... · PITCHING WOO... · PIZZA BALL · PLATE... AR... GE...

...UDSON · ROCK PILE · ROCKEFELLER · ROCKET MAN · ROLLERCOASTER · ROMMEL · ROODLE · ROSEAN...
...E OPERATION · SANDBAGGER · SANDY · SAUCE · SAUDI-ARABIA · SAW · SAYONARA! · SCHWAG (C...
...RVICE ENTRANCE · SEVEN-UP · SHAGGING · SHANK · SHAPIRO · SHEDDY · SHOOT (TO) · SHORT GAM...
...SKINNY · SKULL · SKYBALL · SKYWRITING · SLAM DUNK · SLICK-SLACKS · SLIDER · SLOOK · SMILE...
...ARME... SNAP-HOOK ...RIPE · SNOWMAN · SNUGGLE ...OFTBALL · SO...TY · SOLID · SOUTH AMERI...
...(THE F... ...AY) · SP... ...SPRAY · SQUIBB · S...AKE IT (T... ...STICK · ST... ...OGIE SOAKER · STONE...
...O · S...NG · SW... ...AP · TARZAN · TAXI... · TEASER · ...MP... A · TEN... ...VE P...OD · TESTER · TE...

...TER! · WATER-BALL · WATERY GRAVE · WATER WEDGE · WHACK · WEDGEWOOD · WHEELS (COMIN...

Let the Big Dog Eat!

Let the Big

COMPILED BY HUBERT PEDROLI

ILLUSTRATED BY MARY TIEGREEN

A WELCOME BOOK

WILLIAM MORROW
NEW YORK

Dog Eat!

A Dictionary of the Secret Language of Golf

Acknowledgements

Our thanks go to Lena Tabori, Hiro Clark, Natasha Fried, and Elizabeth Kessler of Welcome Enterprises for getting us a tee time. To Jacqueline Deval of Hearst Books for insisting on picking up the green fees. To Tony Scheitinger, Christopher Young, and Muriel Allen for their skills with the graphite shaft. And to Angela Ramirez, Gustavo Escalante, and Dave Green for their graphic and production skills.

So many friends contributed words, images, and moral support. In no particular order (certainly not handicap) our thanks to Dave Green (again), John Elliott, and Bob Irish, all three of them hard-core dimpleheads; Milbry Polk for her support and patience; Joe, Barry, and Katie Hyde, a dangerous lot with clubs in hand (not to mention forks and knifes); The Johnson brothers, Alan, Tom, and Bruce. Their mother, Genevieve, was a serious golfer who made sure her sons never followed in her tragic path; dear Betty Goodman from Detroit; super-models Bobby Griffin, Tony Acosta, Dr. Phillip Bauman, Gary White, Jimmy Webb, Robin Siegel, and Marielle Staub; Jin Kim, a man never pressed for words; Kings of "The Hill" Bernie Doyle, Dave Englander, and John Morgan; The Jones of Legend Trail (who contributed no less than "Dogballs"); Brennen Pfiefer of Westin Mission Hills Golf Resort who added to the "J's"; the amazing George and Susan Lewis of Golfiana; our wise and wonderful friends at the Ralph Miller Golf Library, Marge Dewey and Saundra Scheffer; Philippe and Sophie Pedroli, and especially Andre "Arnie" Pedroli,

who, from very early on, taught his son how *not* to play golf; to Janet O'Meara for her love of the game, and to E.E. Tiegreen for his love of words.

And finally, to Daisy, a big dog who is always ready to eat, we dedicate this book.

Introduction

Golf has to be, by far, the most challenging game ever designed by Man. Chess may demand more brains, and yachting is slightly more pricey, bungee jumping requires more courage. But none can compare to the challenge of golf. First you have to pay zillions of dollars to buy clubs and take at least two forty-dollar lessons. Then you have to hit hundreds of buckets of balls at the driving range and watch countless hours of video-tapes purchased on late-night infomercials. You find the right logo shirt and the lucky pants, attach the soft spikes and arrange your weapons. Finally, on a glorious spring morning, you declare yourself ready for battle.

On the first tee you survey the landscape. Upon asking the distance to the hole, your golfing partner answers: "A *buck and a half* to the *cat box*. It's in the *jungle book*." And you thought you knew golf!

Alas, there is one part of the game they don't teach you in golf school, not even in the video-tapes. Hitting the ball 300 yards is the easy part. You may be able to walk the golf walk, but you've also got to talk the golf talk. Swing, club, and ball might be the first three golf words a novice golfer might learn, but the odds are that green will not be the next. *Worm-burner* is more likely, or perhaps *whiff*, *chunk*, or *blow-dry*.

Precision is as fundamental to golf as the parachute is to sky-diving. A deviation in the golf swing of an eighth of an inch can mean the difference between hitting a *happy* and a *chunky tuna*. And the language of golf is no exception. Understanding the difference between a *Liz Taylor* and a *Linda Ronstadt* is crucial to communication.

Do not despair. Help is here at last. From *A-game* to *Zorro*, we present the indispensable dictionary for the renaissance golfer.
Let the Big Dog Eat!

THE SECRET LANGUAGE OF GOLF

A description of a typical round, as told to the author by a fellow golf enthusiast.

The dawn patrol was on the 16th tee. Jimbo (who'd been dialing 8 all morning) decided to let the big dog eat. "Jack it up, Birdie Boy!" said the Donmeister, hoping to exert some psychological pressure. Jimbo held an impromptu ground breaking ceremony with his pitching wood, and unleashed a rainmaker that crash landed O.B. Electing to take his mulligan, Jimbo reloaded. Unfortunately, the wheels had come off by that time, and he foozled. That ball was gonzo and Jimbo had to go backpacking in the mahoofka.

Meanwhile, the Donmeister (pleased to see Jimbo's ABFU), hit a smoker right down the pipe. Out on the fluffy with a buck and a half to the dance floor!

Next up was Nick, (who had carded dog balls on 15). He was snake bit on the front and ever since his beagle on 10, he'd been choking. Nick pulled out the furniture and hit a porker into the cabbage.

Last on deck was Bernie, who always tried to kill the ball. Today was no different, except this time he connected, hit it flush, and launched an F-14. Bernie's ball was a Linda Ronstadt, and made the Donmeister extremely nervous. He searched in his pocket for the old equalizer.

Bernie and the Donmeister got in their chariot and took off down the runway, while Nature Boy and the rough rider conducted a rescue operation in the mahoofka.

Jimbo had an iffy lie, but was able to clip the ball. Now back on the short grass, he would have a chance at saving par. Unfortunately, Nick was playing Oprah golf and hit a humiliating grass cutter. His next shot was a blow dry, followed by a chili-dip. Unable to get off the Bogey train, Nick wiped the klingons from his blade and pocketized his ball. He returned to the BIPmobile, bagging the hole.

Bernie's second shot was more in character, and he hit a toe jam that landed him in jail.

The quench wench arrived with the gut truck, and Nick (the keg man) purchased a round of aiming fluid. Now loosened up with swing oil, Jimbo hit a screamer that landed 100 yards from the green.

The Donmeister managed to hit a Yasir Arafat. Now facing a fried egg, he grabbed his spatula and airmailed the green, again landing on the beach. The Donmeister spent the next ten minutes looking for Pamela Anderson. He finally escaped from the cat box and onto the carpet, only to fall prey to a bad case of the yips. The Donmeister was on the top shelf, a long way from the barn, and considering the break, he needed to borrow at least six feet. He zapped a putt that rolled ten feet past the can. The Donmeister couldn't stop the bleeding. His next putt had a case of liprosy and it did a paint job. He finally hit a tap in and carded a snowman.

Bernie had escaped from the jungle with a little help from the old foot mashie. Now on the brillo, he pulled out the Texas wedge and jammed one in the jar for par. "You da man!" he thought to himself.

Jimbo hit it flush, and cozied it up to the pin. Finally, he drained his knee-knocker and ended up with a respectable bogey. While Jimbo and Bernie decided to go for an emergency nine, Nick remained BIPSIC and the Donmeister went to hit fungoes on murderers' row.

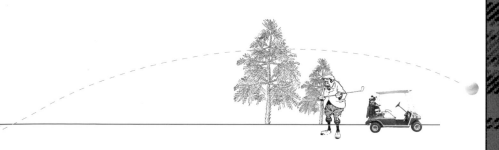

AFTER AN AIR BALL, MR. KIM GETS AN ACE.

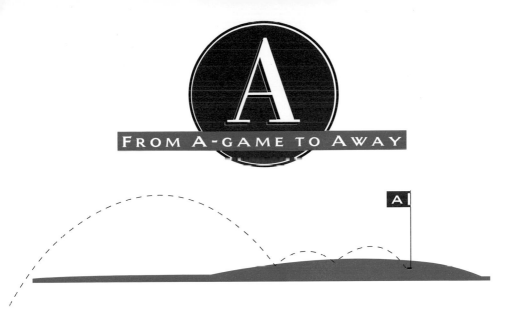

A-game: A rare state of peak golfing performance. As in: "We're playing Sawgrass next weekend. Bring your *A-game* and a dozen extra balls."

aboard: The desirable position of being on the green.

ABSU: Acronym for After Birdie Screw Up. A debilitating psycho-physiological ailment afflicting millions of golfers. A common *ABSU* is a triple-bogey following a birdie. Synonym: *ABFU*.

ace: In theory, an ace is just a hole in one. Real life on the golf course can be more complex, even paradoxical, as seen in the following example: "At the 3rd hole, a 155-yard par-3, Winthrop skulled his first shot into the water, but he *aced* his second shot to save par."

action: A common word for backspin. (Also see *full flaps, moonwalking.*)

adios: Spanish for good-bye. Frequently used in the proximity of a rio. (Also see *AMF ball.*)

adrenaline: What TV commentators say is flowing in the veins of a pro who overshoots the green.

aerosol man: A golfer who sprays a lot.

afraid of the dark: When a putt comes to the edge of the hole and decides to either stop short or proceed past the cup.

ahead: To *get ahead of the ball* describes the heinous situation when the golfer casts his or her body forward on the downswing instead of staying "behind" the ball. Results vary from a benign skull to a catastrophic shank. *I got ahead of it* is a handy excuse to dispense for any poorly executed shot.

aiming fluid: Alcoholic beverage such as beer or whiskey consumed while playing. (Also see *quench wench, swing oil.*)

air ball: Also known as an air-shot, it is a stroke that misses the ball entirely. As in "Mrs. Roberston hit an air ball off the 1st tee, but she declared it was only a practice shot." (Also see *blow dry, drive-by shooting, whiff.*)

#@%*§#∅@&!

BEFORE   AFTER

THE AIR BALL

Air-Canada: A funny thing to say when your opponent's tee-shot sails into foreign territory. (See *zip code.*)

airmail the green (to): To fly over and well past the green. As in: "Francis hit a beautiful wedge at the 9th, but somehow his ball *airmailed the green* and broke the windshield of a Mercedes-Benz in the parking lot."

air press: A press, or bet, made on a single hole while the ball is still airborne. Doesn't work with worm-burners.

albatross: Three strokes under par on a hole. This very rare bird is also known as a double eagle.

Alice: Ralph Cramden's wife in *The Honeymooners* TV series. Also, an affectionate way to speak to your ball on the putting green, especially when it stops short of the hole: "Oh *Alice!*" No relation to Pete Dye's wife.

all square: In match play, when the two players are even, the match is said to be *all square.*

amateur side: On a slanted green, the side below the hole. Supposedly where most weekend golfers will miss their putts.

AMF ball: A famous brand of golf balls designed for playing over water hazards. (Adios, My Friend!)

angel gooser: A very high drive. (See *Ascending Tee Shots* diagram on page 40.)

apron: The tightly mowed area that surrounds the green. See *skirt, brillo.*

Archie: A ball that ends up in a bunker. (See *Golf Celebrities* box on page 48.)

army golf: Also known as military golf or marine corps golf, it describes a style of play which favors an indirect route to the green: left, right, left, right. (Also see *Z-golf, Zorro.*)

around the world: A score of 80. A far-fetched reference to great science-fiction author Jules Verne's novel *Around The World in 80 Days.*

au revoir: French for good-bye. Used immediately after hitting the ball in the general direction of a water hazard. In France, golf etiquette requires that you remove your beret when saying *au revoir.*

ARMY GOLF

Audi: A score of 4. Clever automotive reference to the Audi Quattro. (See *The Numbers of Golf* box on page 76.)

auditor: The fellow in your foursome who keeps re-counting your strokes.

avalanche shot: A shot from a highly elevated tee on a par-3 with no fairway between tee and green.

away: The third of golf's three most hated words. (Also see *USA.*)

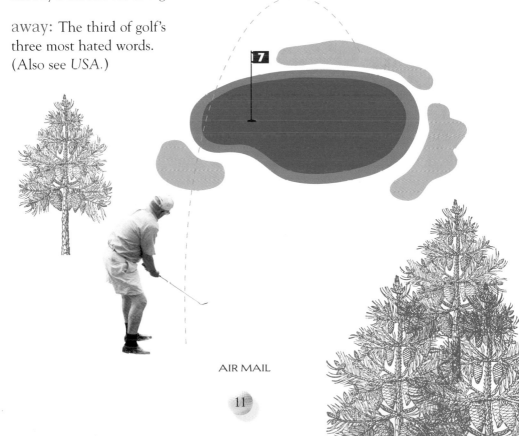

AIR MAIL

back: The back tees. As in "Last week end I played the Monster from all the way *back* and none of my tee shots reached the fairway." Also known as the tips, tiger tees.

back door: The far side of the hole.

back nine: The final nine holes. As in "The *back nine* at the Vulcan Mines Golf Course is really only eight holes since the 12th fairway disappeared in the sink hole tragedy of 1986."

backpacking: When a player spends a lot of time in the rough, he or she is said to be backpacking. As in: "Since Mrs. Peper went *backpacking* for the entire length of the 7th hole, everyone was surprised to hear her announce a par."

back side: A rude way of referring to the back nine.

back stalls: The back stalls are the back tees. Also known as the *blues*, *blue plates*, *tiger tees*, and *tips*.

bacon strip: A long, thin divot that ranges in size from 5″ to 7″ and never more than 2″ in width. As in: "Frank is a very technical player. He studies his *bacon strips* after each fat shot." (See *The Dirt on Divots*, page 32.)

baffie: In the olden days, a highly-lofted wood club. The modern equivalent would be a 5-wood.

bag (to bag a hole): To skip a hole. As in: "Murray was two shots down when he declared that he was late for a bar mitzvah and had to *bag* the last two holes."

bag (to be on the bag): To caddie for in pro-tour lingo. As in: "Angelo was *on Jack's bag* for years, but he eventually retired and opened a restaurant in Miami."

bag (to have a shot in the bag): To have a shot in one's repertoire. For example, when facing a side-hill three-iron shot to an elevated green, "I know I have the *shot in my bag*, but the question is can I pull it off today?"

bag line: What golfers waited on before tee times were invented.

bag rat: A young caddie. As in: "Dr. Bauman's wife always chooses the bag rat with the sensitive eyes." Also known as bird dog, flag waver, looper.

bail out (to): 1) To hit away from a dangerous hazard, as in: "In his attempt to *bail out* to the right of the pond, Herb sliced his tee shot and went out of bounds." 2) To escape from, as in: "Herb had just *bailed out* from the fairway bunker when he sliced his approach and went out of bounds."

bald eagle: A hair shy of an eagle.

baldy: Another term for an eagle. At some clubs it is also the nickname of the oldest member.

ball-hawker: A person always looking for lost balls. Ball-hawkers keep score a different way. For example: "Joe Hyde is a champion *ball-hawker*. Today he lost 10 balls but found 13, for a net score of 3."

balloon (to): A shot balloons when the ball climbs out of control into the wind. For example: "At Ballybunion's 12th hole, Phil's tee shot ballooned into the wind and we all ran for cover."

banana ball: For right handed players, a shot with a vicious left-to-right trajectory. The other way around for southpaws. No relation to the orange golf ball. (Also see *chiquita*.)

Band-Aid: A golf swing remedy hastily devised on the golf course. (Also see *bleeding*.)

bank shot: Terminology borrowed from pool. A shot that bounces off some mound or elevation and returns to the fairway. For example: "Betty tried a *bank shot* at the 5th hole, but the ball vanished into the woods and she had a crying fit."

BANANA BALL

banker: A bad player who keeps winning.

barbecuing it: To hit a great drive. Same as smoking it.

barber: A golfer who uses questionable math to shave strokes off his score (Also see *equalizer*, *fudge factor*.)

bare lie: A grassless lie. (Also see *hardpan lie*, *naked lie*.)

barkie: A par made after hitting a tree. For example: "Tom was unbelievably lucky today. He had two *barkies*, two splashies and one sheddy. I'll never play with him again." (Also see *bowker*.)

barrel: The hole, especially when the putt goes in. (Also see *can*, *cup*, *jar*, *tin*.)

beach (the): A bunker or sand trap. A popular destination for weekend golfers.

beach ball: A ball that has landed in a bunker.

beach party: A social event taking place when two or more players meet at the same beach.

beagle: A score of double par, often committed with the help of the big dog.

beaned (to get): To be hit in the head by a stray golf ball. As in: "Jack was innocently relieving himself in the woods when he got *beaned* by a ball coming from the 14th fairway."

beat balls (to): To hit practice shots at the driving range. Golf legend Ben Hogan was the first professional to understand the importance of *beating balls*.

beaver pelt: A type of divot. Unlike the thin and narrow bacon strip, the *beaver pelt* is wide, thick, and heavy. The best *beaver pelts* are harvested with a sand wedge when the fairway is wet. (See *The Dirt on Divots*, page 32.)

THE BELLY SNAP

bell ringer: A shot that hits the flagstick and makes a ringing sound.

belly it: When the clubhead makes unintentional contact with the belly of the ball, just below the equator. The result in a nauseatingly low-flying shot.

belly shot: A delicate chip shot where the ball is struck like a putt, but with the bottom edge of a sand wedge. Pros like Craig Stadler can hit the *belly shot*. The average golfer can't. (Also see *skull*.)

belly snap: When a player with a paunch gets it all into the shot. Before attempting to combine the *belly snap* with a two-checker, it is advisable to consult your swing doctor.

belt (to): To hit a big drive. As in: "At the ladies' championship, Mrs. Jones *belted* one 30 yards past Mrs. Cunningham."

bend (to): To intentionally hit a shot that curves to the right or left. For example: "To *bend* his drive to the left, Glen used a strong grip and hooded the club face, but surprisingly, that was the best shot he hit all day and his ball went straight into the lake."

big dog: The driver. As in: "Come on Margie, not that seven-wood again! Why don't you *let the big dog eat* once in a while?" Sometimes referred to as *letting the big dog bark*. (Also see *Chief, lumber*.)

THE BIG DOG

bikini wax: Famous expression once used by pro-golfer turned maverick TV commentator Gary McCord, to describe the green-mowing technique used at the Augusta National. Unlike the rest of us, Masters officials were not amused. (See *Long-Eared Society*.)

2

BEANED

bingo bango bongo: A game in which three points are awarded for each hole: first on the green (*Bingo*); closest to the hole (*Bango*); and first in the hole (*Bongo*). Although this in not truly golf slang, it is included here simply because it is so much fun to say. Can also go under the name of bingle bangle bongle.

BIP*MOBILE*

BIP: Acronym for Ball In Pocket. BIP generally occurs before reaching the green and results in an X on the scorecard.

BIPmobile: Personal transportation for one or more BIPSIC players.

BIPSIC: Acronym for Ball In Pocket/Sulking In Cart. A state of angry depression commonly experienced after hitting back-to-back out-of-bounds or triple chili-dipping. Do not try humor with a BIPSIC person. Only time can heal BIPSIC.

bird dog: A caddie, especially if he is good at finding balls in the rough. Also referred to as a bag rat, flag waver, looper.

birdie: Everybody knows that one.

Birdie Boy (or Girl): The person who had a birdie on the previous hole and now has the honors on the tee. Calling someone a *Birdie Boy* is intended to put subtle pressure on him and hopefully provoke an ABSU or ABFU.

BLASTING OFF THE BEACH

birdie territory: 1) The region close enough to the hole to have a reasonable chance at making a birdie. 2) An Audubon-certified golf course.

bisque: A handicap stroke that can be taken anywhere during a round. No one uses that word anymore .

Bitc!: What some players say after skulling a chip. (Also see *Marv Albert*.)

blade: An iron. As in: "Frank paid $800 for a new set of *blades*, but the swing looks like the old one to me."

blade it: To hit a thin shot, with a low slicing trajectory. As in: "During the pro-am, the Vice President *bladed* a two-iron into the gallery."

A BLADE

blast (to): 1) A type of bunker shot which sends a large amount of sand and gravel onto the green, occasionally accompanied by the ball. 2) To hit the ball with a powerful swing, as in: "While playing in the Acme Plumbing Supplies Annual Golf Outing, Rob *blasted* a huge drive over the dogleg's corner and hit his boss who was playing in the foursome ahead."

bleeding (to be): When a player suffers a series of bad strokes or holes. For example: "After a nice 45 on the front nine, Al started *bleeding* with double-bogeys on 11, 12 and 13. When he made a triple on 14, he picked up and headed straight for the emergency room." (See *Band-Aid, emergency room, hospital zone, recovery room*.)

blood (no): In match play, the expression *no blood* indicates there was no winner or loser on the hole, and thus no money won or lost. Note: As long as your opponent *bleeds* as much as you do, there's still *no blood*.

blow dry: An air shot. *Blow-drys* are often mislabeled as practice swings. (Also see *drive-by shooting, whiff*.)

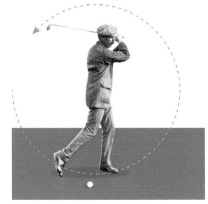

blue plates: The back tees, which are often indicated with blue markers.

blueprint (to): To execute a shot precisely as it should be played, i.e., according to the plan.

A BLOW DRY

blues (the): Refers to the blue markers, which used to be the farthest back on the tee. Playing from the *blues* has several advantages: fewer divots, often a nicer view, more golf course for the money and too far back to reach any hazards. These days, the blues can be called black, gold, Championship, tiger, pro or just about anything else. The opposite of *blue* is red. (Also see *tips*.)

Bo Derek: 1) A term used to describe a perfect shot, in reference to her famous film role as the perfect woman. 2) A score of 10 on a hole. In this case, far from perfect.

bogey dust: The sand.

Bogeyland: An area of the course often frequented by the Bogeyman. (See *Bogeyman*.)

Bogeyman: A relative of Old Man Par, but not as elusive. As in: "Jack was even par on the front nine, but tragically, right after the turn, he ran smack into the *Bogeyman*."

bogey train (to be on the): To be unable to score anything but bogeys. As in: "Scott finally made par at the 9th hole, but after downing a hot dog and a brewski at the turn, he hopped back onto the *bogey train*."

bolo ball: A style of play where the ball is mostly hit along the ground.

bomb: A long drive with a high trajectory. Unlike in life or in the theatre, in golf a *bomb* is a good thing. (Also see *cream, crunch, F-14, kill, smoke*.)

boomerang: A putt that comes back at you after rolling around the rim.

borrow: The amount of distance to the right or left of the cup that one must aim to account for the breaks on a green. As in: "The green was so sloped that Mr. Schneckler had to *borrow* six feet on his putt, which happily ended up as a toilet flusher.

Boss of the Moss: Pro tour lingo for a very good putter. Can be used at the country club, too, as in: "Mrs. Fennigan was *Boss of the Moss* today. She three-putted only thrice."

bowker: A shot that bounces off a tree or a spectator and lands back in the fairway. As in: "While in the pro-am, the Vice-President got four *bowkers*, including a barky and a sheddy."

BORROW

GOLF ARCHITECTURE: A PRIMER

A good golf architect must know how to blend natural and man-made elements to create a layout which is both beautiful and challenging. From the tips to the dance floor, the designer must use great skill and flair in selecting the right location for cat boxes, the jungle, and the drink. Too much spinach will slow down play, not enough mahoofka makes for a dull round. Below is a schematic diagram of a typical golf hole containing some of the natural and man-made features found on fine courses everywhere.

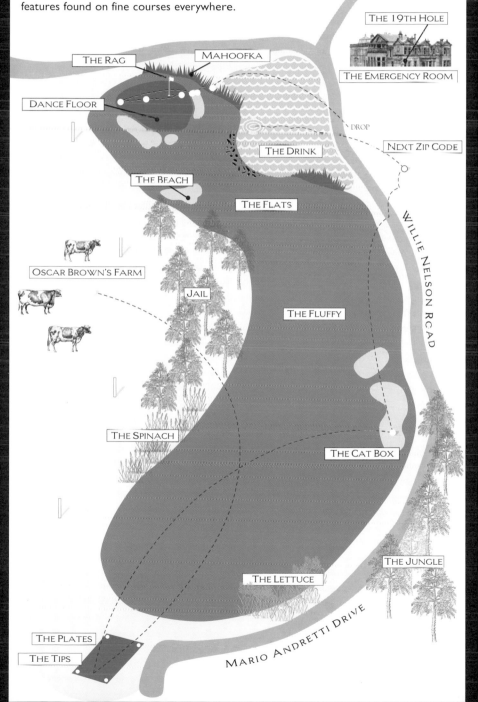

THE 19TH HOLE

THE EMERGENCY ROOM

THE RAG

MAHOOFKA

DANCE FLOOR

DROP

NEXT ZIP CODE

THE DRINK

THE BEACH

THE FLATS

OSCAR BROWN'S FARM

JAIL

THE FLUFFY

WILLIE NELSON ROAD

THE SPINACH

THE CAT BOX

THE JUNGLE

THE LETTUCE

THE PLATES

THE TIPS

MARIO ANDRETTI DRIVE

bowling: To mark an X on the scorecard.

bowling lane: A narrow fairway. (Also see *gutter ball*.)

boy scout (to): To hit a shot with a full swing. As in: "On his approach shot at the ninth, George *boy scouted* a six-iron and landed in the clubhouse dining room."

brag tags: Plastic tag indicating that you have left your personal divot on an expensive track. Common brag tags: Pebble Beach, TPC at Sawgrass, PGA West. Example of highly-prized *brag tag*: Worn-out Pine Valley member tag.

brainer: A skulled shot. As in: "Jane was only 50 yards short of the green in two, but then she hit three consecutive *brainers* with her wedge."

break: The slant of the putting surface between the ball and the hole. As in: "The *breaks* on Pinehurst No. 2's greens are so severe, you might as well putt with a wedge."

breakfast ball: Another term for a Mulligan.

break some eggs (to): To hit practice balls. (See *rockpile*.)

brillo: The short grass around the green. (Also see *fringe, skirt, froghair*.)

broom: To hit a putt with a low, sweeping motion. (See *broomstick*.)

broomstick: The long putter. As in: "Following a disastrous putting streak, Miss Dalrymple shocked everyone by showing up with a *broomstick* at the next ladies' outing."

bubble (to be on the): Tour lingo. A pro uncertain of making the cut at a tournament is "on the bubble." As in: "Arnie was *on the bubble* on Friday afternoon, but charged back and marched to victory on Sunday."

buck (a): Informal way of describing a distance of 100 yards. An example would be, when asked the distance to the pin: "From here, a *buck* and a half, maybe a *buck* sixty."

Buckshot Billy: Any player for whom accuracy is not a strong point.

bug-cutter: An unintentional, low trajectory shot. For example: "Miss Kessler certainly hit her share of bug-cutters today." (See *Low Shots Diagram*, page 92.)

buried lie: A ball almost completely entombed in the sand. (See *The Lies of Golf*, page 21.)

burn the hole (to): A putt that rolls over the rim but keeps going *burns the hole*.

bush-blaster: A big drive that flies hard into the trees. As in: "Frank hit a real *bush-blaster* at the 13th. He went looking for his ball and was never to be seen again."

butter knife: The one-iron, when they still made them. For example: "Peter chose the *butter knife* at the 235-yard, par-3 10th, and, had it not been for the pond in front of the tee, his ball could have rolled all the way to the green."

buzzard: An old-fashioned word for a double-bogey. It's a good word. Bobby Jones used it in his books.

bye: The remaining hole(s) after a match has been won, often played as a new game.

bye bye!: Last two words heard before "Splash!"

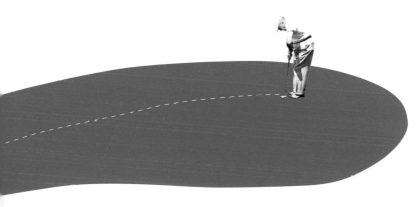

BOSS OF THE MOSS

21

cabbage pounder: A player who spends a lot of time in the rough, also known as the cabbage. As in: "Dave, Joe, Bernie, and Herb are just a bunch of *cabbage pounders.*"

caddie swing: A flat swing.

Cadillac Strut: A swinging, nonchalant style of walking to the cup after making a long putt. Especially effective while wearing pastel slick slacks.

camel (a): A player who spends a lot of time in the sand.

can (the): The not particularly poetic but visually correct designation for the hole. (Also see *barrel, cup, jar, tin.*)

can (to): To make a putt. As in: "Fred *canned* a three-footer to save double bogey."

candles: A score of eleven. Also called candlesticks.

candy: Any sort of prize won on a hole. For example: "Jimbo had to fork over some major *candy* after the Donmeister sank an ocean liner on 14." Also known as *junk.*

Captain Hook: A hook that ends up in the water. Can also refer to the perpetrator.

Captain Kirk: A shot that goes where no man has gone before. As with Captain Hook, the term can also refer to the one performing the act.

Captain Pose: A player who assumes an elegant pose after each shot, regardless of where the ball has gone.

CAPTAIN POSE

22

card (to): To score, or to write on the scorecard. For example: "In spite of several double pars and an unfortunate series of triple bogeys, Dr. Gadziwill *carded* a net 71 at the club championship."

career shot: A once-in a lifetime golf shot. As in: "Mrs. Neidermeier hit a *career shot* at the 18th today. She holed a 90-foot chip from inside the cart garage."

carpet: A finely mowed grassy surface. Usually refers to the green, sometimes to the fairway. (See *dance floor, fluffy.*)

carry: The distance a golf ball flies or needs to fly, as opposed to roll. As in: "Bruce, who sometimes gets carried away, thought he could *carry* the water hazard with his driver. Alas, such was not the case."

cart golf: A style of play invented in America, designed to maximize the expense and minimize the amount of physical exercise.

cart path: Often the last point of contact between a ball and out-of-bounds. (See *Mario Andretti, O'Brien, Oscar Brown.*)

CELLOPHANE BRIDGE

cart-path management: The skill of hitting the ball as close as possible to the cart path. Speeds up play when carts are not allowed on the fairway.

cat box: Sandtrap.

cellophane bridge: An invisible film covering the hole and preventing a perfectly struck putt from going in.

Center City: A shot that goes right down the middle of the fairway is from *Center City*. (Also see *split the fairway.*)

center cut: Pro terminology for a putt that goes straight into the middle of the hole.

Central America: Like it's Latin cousin, the South America, this is a putt that could use just one more revolution. (Also see *The World of Golf* diagram.)

Chainsaw City: A place somewhere in the middle of the jungle. (Also see *The World of Golf* diagram.)

chainsaw lie: The type of lie you get in Chainsaw City.

character builder: The dreaded six-footer: Eminently makeable, yet oh so missable. (See *Putt Measurement* diagram, page 53.)

chariot: Golf cart, as in: "Hop on the *chariot*, Ben! I'll drive you to your ball." (Also see *BIPmobile, hummer*.)

charity ball: A quasi-mulligan. For example: "Linda was so upset after blow-drying her first two shots that the other ladies gave her a *charity ball*."

cheeks (hitting with both): Putting the fatty tissues surrounding the gluteus maximus to maximum use in the golf swing. A two-cheeker is a long, solid drive.

cheerleader: An overdressed, label-conscious golfer. For example: "David is a real *cheerleader*. He's way over the legal logo limit." (See *golf princess*.)

chief (the): The driver. To hit the chief is to use the driver. For example: "You don't need to hit the chief on the 14th hole, a three-wood is enough to go in the water." Also known as big dog, lumber.

HITTING WITH
BOTH CHEEKS

chili-dipping: When the club makes contact with the ground before the ball. *Chili-dipping* is not good for your golf health. The USGA recommends that fat shots make up less than 20% of your golf diet. (See *Fat Shots*, page 38.)

chippie: A chip that goes in the hole. Usually worth a dollar.

chiquita (a): Slice named for its resemblance to the shape of the tropical fruit. Also called banana ball.

choke (to): To hit a bad shot due to psychological pressure. As in: "Caspar thought he had lost the match after he *choked* and drove into the jungle at the 15th. Fortunately for him, however, Marcel *choked* even more and ran out of balls at the 16th."

choke down (to): To grip the club one or several inches lower than normal. As in: "I *choked down* on a wedge to get out off the mahoofka, but, sad to say, I chunked it anyway."

choker: Somebody who has a habit of choking. Calling somebody a *choker* is a grave golf insult. All golfers are, have been or will be *chokers*.

chop: Another word for a hacker or unskilled golfer. As in: "It took us five hours to play 18 holes this afternoon! We were stuck behind a bunch of *chops*!" Also known as a *dub, duffer, hacker,* or *mudder*.

chopper: A helicopter-like practice swing where the club does not stop at the finish but continues overhead and returns to address in a single, uninterrupted motion. Again, don't try this in front of the mirror.

chop shot: A short, little shot with no follow-through. May be voluntary or not. Unrelated to the chops mentioned above.

chowder it (to): Same as chili-dipping before Taco Bell invaded the suburbs.

chubby: A shot that's a little bit fat.

chuck wagon: The beverage cart. As in: "I hope Denise is driving the *chuck wagon* this afternoon!" Also known as a *gut truck*.

chunk: Means pretty much what it sounds like. If the divot flies farther than the ball, it is an indication that you *chunked* it. (See *Fat Shots*, page 38.)

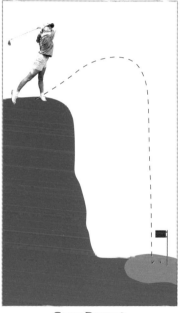

CLIFF DIVING

chunky tuna: A chunked shot that ends up in a water hazard.

clear-cutting: Illegal and morally repugnant practice of whacking the tall grass, weeds, and branches surrounding your ball in the rough. Best done with a wedge.

cleats: Slang for golf shoes. (Also see *spikes*.)

cliff diving: To hit a shot from a highly elevated tee.

clip (to clip the ball): To sweep the ball cleanly off the ground without making contact with the turf or sand. As in: "Mrs. Wong's seven-iron *clipped* the ball neatly off the sand, but she had no time to yell 'Fore!' and the ball struck Miss Baysinger on the rump."

clock (on the): Pro-tour expression. A player or group of players officially warned for slow play are said to be *on the clock*.

clock (to): To hit a powerful, long drive. As in "Gee, Phil, you really clocked that one. You're all the way past the ladies' tee."

clutcher: A key golf shot on which victory or defeat hinges. As in: "The *clutcher* was when, for the first time that day, Dorothy made a two-footer at the 16th."

coal shovel: The sand wedge. As in: "Honey, could you hand me my *coal-shovel*, please?"

collar: Shortly-mowed grass area leading to the green.

comebacker: A great putt following a terrible one. As in: "Mrs. Fluggendorf made the mother of all *comebackers* this afternoon. She holed out a 50-footer after missing a steep downhill *tap-in*."

commercial shot: A low-risk shot designed to win rather than convince.

company balls: Range balls.

condo golf: A style of golf derived from the Royal and Ancient game, where the rough and water hazards have been replaced by patio furniture and swimming pools. Popular in Florida.

connect (to): A pleasurable but fleeting sensation of transcendental communication between mind, body, club, and ball.

cow pasture: A poorly-maintained, uninteresting golf course. What Sam Snead called St. Andrews' Old Course on his first visit. Similar to a dog track.

cozy it up: To hit an approach shot extremely close to the pin, say one to three feet. (See *nestle, snuggles*.)

crafted: Adjective used to described a chip or putt of artistic quality. The word is generally accompanied by the adverb finely. As in: "Mrs Boatwater saved bogey with a *finely crafted* chip from behind the ball washer."

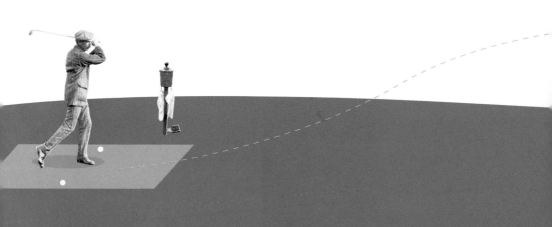

cream (to): To strike very hard. Usually applies to a putt that overshoots the hole by six feet or more. As in: "Wayne *creamed* his putt on 12 and ended up looking for Pamela Anderson."

crop duster: A shot that travels about head-high. (See *Fore!*)

croquet: A refined lawn game sometimes played on the golf course.

crunch (to): To hit a powerful, straight tee shot. For example: "Gilbert *crunched* a 280-yard drive at the 10th, but then he chunked his wedge-shot and threw the guilty club into the lake".

cub scout: To hit a shot with less than a full swing. As in: "Walking up the 18th fairway towards the clubhouse, so keen was George to avoid a repeat of his earlier tragedy on the adjacent 9th, that he decided to *cub scout* a seven-iron and ended up carding a Bo Derek."

Culligan: A mulligan that ends up in the water. (See *mulligan, shapiro.*)

cup: The hole. Also known as the barrel, jar, or tin.

cuppy lie: A ball resting at the bottom of a small depression.

curler: A short putt with a lot of break. As in: "Herb's second putt was an easy three-foot downhill *curler*, but unfortunately he got a case of the *yips* and found himself 30 feet away for his third."

Cut!: A plea addressed to a ball that's heading to the left.

cut shot: A shot with an intentional left-to-right trajectory. Right-to-left for lefties. (Also see *fade, pizza ball, serving cake.*)

Cutty Sark: Pro slang for a cut shot. As in: "Give it a little *Cutty Sark*, Lee!"

A CULLIGAN

DANCING ON THE LINE

dance floor: The putting green. As in: "Cindy was on the *dance floor*, but at 40 feet from the cup, she was too far away to hear the music."

dancing on the line: The repulsing act of walking between another player's ball and the cup. As in: "Jimbo missed the six-footer he needed for a double-bogey and accused Mary Lou of having danced on his line."

Darth Fader: A fearsome slicer. (Also see *fade*.)

DAP: Acronym for Dead-Ass Perfect. An excellent shot.

DAS: Dead-Ass Solid. A cousin of *DAP*.

dawn patrol: The first foursome to get out on the course in the morning. They tend to belong to one of the following categories: friends or relatives of the head-pro; current or former town employees; computer hackers or dimpleheads who slept in the parking lot. (See *dimplehead*.)

dead: Approach shot that stops inches away from the hole. As in: "Our approaches were both *dead* at the 18th, but suddenly there was lightning in the sky, and we picked up our balls and ran inside for we did not want to suffer the same fate."

dead cat: A sizeable divot, somewhat wider than a bacon strip but not as large as a beaver pelt. (See *The Dirt on Divots*, page 30.)

Declaration of Independence: A score of 76.

deuce: The two-iron. As in: "This hole is a bowling lane. I'd rather hit the *deuce* than the lumber."

dew sweepers: The first players on the course in the morning. (See *dawn patrol, dimplehead.*)

dialing 8: To hit the ball a long distance, referring to the necessity to dial 8 in many hotels in order to make a long-distance call. As in: "Bubba was *dialing* 8 all day, but he ran out of change at the 13th and made a local call into the lake."

DIMPLEHEADS ON THE PAR-2 COURSE

dimplehead: A golfer who will do anything to fulfill his passion for the game. Among other things, a *dimplehead* plays in the rain and in frigid weather, buys game-improvement gizmos from catalogs and TV infomercials, collects and displays logo balls and goes to Myrtle Beach at least once a year.

dimple pimple (a): A blemish or a scratch on a golf ball.

dink (a): A skulled shot that rolls only a few yards.

direct deposit: A pitch or a chip that goes in the hole.

divorce court: A match where husband and wife (or significant others) play together.

dog (a): A terrible shot.

DIRECT DEPOSIT

dog balls: A score of 8. (See *snowman*.)

dog golf: Canine-style golf, where the player goes from tree to tree.

dogleg: A hole is termed a dogleg if it bends to the right or left. A *dogleg* right is sometimes called a Rover, and a *dogleg* left is a Lassie.

dog track: A poorly maintained golf course. (See *cow pasture*.)

Dolly Parton: A putt that seems fascinated by the size of the cup before going in.

dormie (to be): Important golf word whose origin is lost in the dark, cobwebbed corridors of golf history. Please consult a serious golf dictionary.

double bogey: Two over par on a given hole. This dangerous condition can lead to BIPSIC. Consult a swing doctor.

double-breaker: A putt that breaks, or turns, right, then left or vice versa.

double buzzard: Prehistoric bird akin to the pterodactyl. May want to check Audubon-certified courses.

double Chen: A double hit, when the club head makes contact with the ball twice during the same shot. (See *T.C Chen*.)

double dog balls: A score of 88. Also called a double snowman or frog eyes.

double golf sticks: 77

double Laurel: A score of 11. Also called candles. (See also *Laurel and Hardy*.)

double looper: A caddie who carries two bags at once.

double par: A 6 on a par 3, 8 on a par 4, 10 on a par 5.

double snowman: A score of 88. Also known as double dog balls or frog eyes.

Doug Sanders (a): A well-dressed golfer who plays poorly. A mean reference to golf great Doug Sanders, who once owned over 300 pair of outlandish golf shoes and sadly lost the 1968 British Open by missing a 2-footer on the 18th.

drain (to): To make a long, serpentine putt. (See *plumber*.)

THE DIRT ON DIVOTS

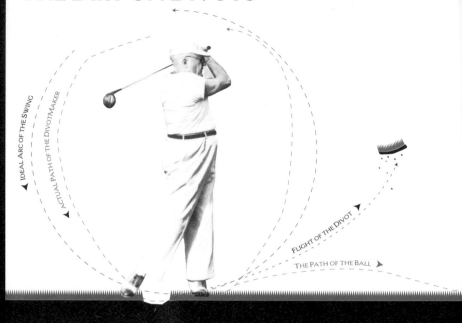

A small deviation from the ideal arc of the swing may result in a variety of flying turf. Scottish in origin, divots are as old as the Royal and Ancient game itself. There are those who argue that the divot is the piece of airborne sod, while traditionalists insist that the true divot is the negative space left in the ground. This fascinating paradox may never be solved. What we do know about divots is their official categories as stipulated by the USDA*. Listed below are the six main groups of divot types, with specifications.

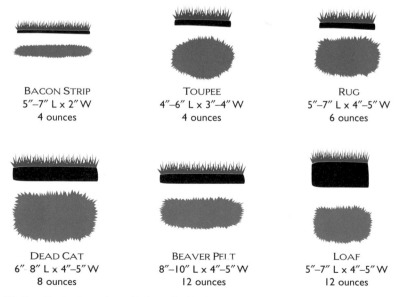

BACON STRIP	TOUPEE	RUG
5"–7" L x 2" W	4"–6" L x 3"–4" W	5"–7" L x 4"–5" W
4 ounces	4 ounces	6 ounces

DEAD CAT	BEAVER PELT	LOAF
6"–8" L x 4"–5" W	8"–10" L x 4"–5" W	5"–7" L x 4"–5" W
8 ounces	12 ounces	12 ounces

* The United States Divot Association is a division of the American Dirt Council.

dribbler: A ball making a humiliating small forward movement following an air shot.

drink (the): A body of water found on a golf course. For example: "Harvey hit a great drive; unfortunately after that he pumped two consecutive five-irons into the *drink*." Lateral *drink* is usually marked by red stakes, frontal by yellow. (Also see *pump*.)

drive-by shooting: A drive that misses the ball entirely. Also called blow dry, whiff. (See *charity ball, mulligan*.)

driving wedge (a): The club used to make an unintentional high, short drive. (See *Ascending Tee Shots* diagram, page 40.)

drown it: To hit the ball into a water hazard.

DSP: Acronym for Dead-Solid Perfect.

dub: Old-fashioned word for a bad golfer. Dubsdread is the name of the championship course at Cog Hill in Chicago.

A DUFFER CAUGHT IN THE ACT OF A DRIVE-BY SHOOTING

dub: A friendly term for the unfriendly double bogey. As in: "Jimbo hit a lateral off the tee and landed in the mahoofka. After an invigorating nature walk and a Yasir Arafat, he four-putted and ended the hole with a *dub*."

duck hook: A grievous shot with a deadly right-to-left trajectory and murderous diving action. Also known as a quacker. (See also *Captain Hook*.)

duffer: A mild, almost endearing word to describe a lousy golfer.

dunk (to): To hit a shot into a water hazard. For example: "Al was going to break 100 for the first time in his life, until he *dunked* three shots into the pond at 18."

dunky: A par salvaged after hitting in a ball into a water hazard. Rare.

Easter egg: A nice, near-new golf ball found in the rough. As in: "Father Gilligan was having bad day on the links until he found a couple of *Easter eggs* near the 12th."

elephant's ass: A high and stinky shot. (See *Ascending Tee Shots* box, page 40.)

EMBO: Early Morning Block Out. Refers to the tendency to push or pull the first few shots after an early tee time.

emergency nine: A quick round of 9 holes. As in: "Bobby and Johnny grabbed a Bud and went for an *emergency nine*, but they got stuck behind a ladies' foursome and their day was ruined."

emergency room: The men's locker room or the bar. (See *nineteenth hole*.)

energizer: A drive that goes on, and on, and on.

equalizer (the old): 1) A favorite putter, as in: "Jimbo was three up, but the Donmeister pulled out *the old equalizer* and evened the match." 2) The eraser on the golf pencil. As in: "The Donmeister was two up but Jimbo pulled out *the old equalizer* and erased his double bogey." Notice how many golf pencils don't have erasers anymore.

Gravel Beach Golf Links		MEADOW VISTA	HOMER'S WAY	INTO THE WOODS	GONE FISHIN	COD DAMMIT	BEAVER'S LAIR	DUCK HOOK	SHANK-RI-LA	HOT DOG CITY	
		1	2	3	4	5	6	7	8	9	OUT
TIPS		407	450	338	569	485	227	401	490	189	3553
WHITE		396	441	330	499	463	204	391	490	189	3357
MIDDLE		375	411	313	474	485	195	381	490	189	3188
LADIES			384	305	446	422	174	312	411	124	2937
MEN'S PAR		4	4	4	5	4	3	4	5	3	36
The Donmeister	4										
Jimbo	4	3	8								
Pierre	5	4	5								
Igor	7	9	11								
LADIES PAR		4	4	4	5	5	3	4	5	3	37
HANDICAP		9	7	13	3	1	15	11	5	17	

THE OLD EQUALIZER

equator: An invisible line that circles the middle of the ball. (See *The World of Golf* map below.)

equatorial: A shot where the ball is struck just below the equator, producing a dangerous, ground-hugging shot.

escape (to): To play a shot out of a trouble spot. For example: "Mrs. Fannisburg hit a gorgeous seven-wood at the 140-yard 6th, but her ball rolled into a deep bunker and after a five-minute sandstorm, she finally *escaped* with a hand-wedge." (See *foot wedge, hand wedge*.)

THE WORLD OF GOLF

The game of golf is international, both in scope and appeal. Below is a map of some of the exciting golf destinations available to players today.

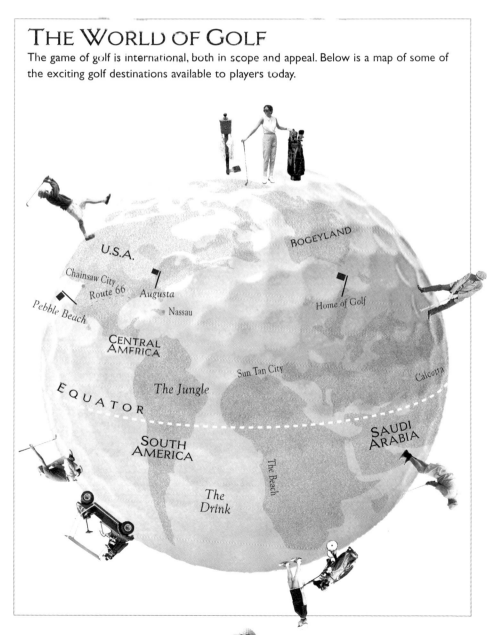

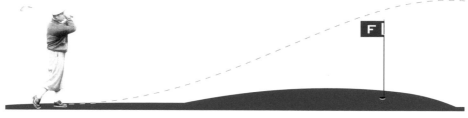

F-14: A drive that takes off like a fighter jet. Related to bomb, cream, crunch, kill, nuke, and smoke.

fade: A shot with a slight left-to-right trajectory, often used as a euphemism for a slice. (Also see *pizza ball, power fade, serving cake*.)

Fast Foot: A player who makes frequent use of the foot-wedge. As in: "Joe is the *fastest foot* east of the Mississippi River."

fat: 1) An unpleasant shot where the club face strikes the turf before the ball. Fat content varies greatly from shot to shot. (See *Fat Shots* diagram, page 38.) 2) The safe part of the green, away from bunkers or water. As in: "Even though Henry hit a fat shot, the ball landed on the *fat* of the green."

Fat City: A favorite weekend golf destination. (See *The World of Golf* box, page 34.)

feather (to): A highly technical stroke producing a lofty trajectory and a soft landing shot. For example: "Mrs. Jasper's attempt to feather a 5-iron onto the Redan green was foiled by the wind, and her ball ended up under a Peugeot in the parking lot."

fighting (a slice or a hook): To battle against the natural tendency of the ball to fly to the right or to the left. For example: "Ben was *fighting* a dreadful slice on the front nine, but after Henry suggested he used a stronger grip he began to snap hook and the two got into a fight."

Fire: To shoot a low score at a tournament. As in: "Annie fired a net 69 at the opening round of the Deadman Gulch's Golf and Gun Club Ladies Championship."

fire at the flag: To aim straight at the hole, as in: "I *fired at the flag* on the island green, but with the Marquis de Sod's pin placement, it never had a chance and went into the drink."

fire away: Military expression inviting a playing companion to tee off first. Often used in combination with Birdie Boy.

first cut: The short rough lining the fairway.

FISA: Acronym for Fudge, I'm Still Away.

fishing rod: A ball retriever. As in: "This course was designed by Pete Dye, and Benny's *fishing rod* came in handy on several holes."

flag: Rectangular piece of fabric hanging from the flagstick. Also known as a rag.

flagstick: The eight-foot pole stuck in the cup that holds the flag. Also called a pin.

flag waver: A caddie. Also referred to as bag rat, bird dog, or looper.

flare: A tee shot that takes off more or less vertically. (See *Ascending Tee Shots* box, page 40.

flat bellies: The younger players on the pro tour. Expression popularized by Lee Trevino. (See *belly shot*, *belly snap*.)

flats: A safe area in the fairway, short of the green and surrounding bunkers.

flat stick: A term for the putter.

flier: A shot hit from the rough which carries and rolls a lot farther than the same shot from the fairway. As in: "Mrs. Lappin says that she prefers to play from the rough because of the *fliers.*"

flog (to play): A backwards version of the Royal and Ancient game.

floof: A bad shot in the days of yore.

flop shot: Basically a sand shot played from a grassy lie. As in: "Dave was practicing his *flop shots* in the backyard when he broke the Garrison's living-room window." Also called a pancake.

16

THE FLOP SHOT

ROSEANNE, LIZ, AND THE CHILI~DIP:
A COMPARISON OF FAT SHOTS

WHILE THE USGA RECOMMENDS AS LITTLE FAT AS POSSIBLE IN THE GOLFER'S DAILY DIET, IT IS AN INESCAPABLE PART OF LIFE ON THE LINKS. FAT SHOTS COME IN MANY VARIETIES, EACH WITH ITS OWN UNIQUE CHARACTERISTICS. SHOWN HERE, IN ASCENDING ORDER OF TROUBLE, ARE: (1) THE *LIZ TAYLOR*, A LITTLE FAT BUT STILL BEAUTIFUL; (2) THE *STUB*, A SHORT BUT GREASY STROKE; (3) THE FAMILIAR *CHUNK* AND (4) THE DISTASTEFUL *CHILI-DIP*; (5) THE *FRITO LAY*, A CHIP HIGH IN DIRT CHOLESTEROL; (6) THE *ROSEANNE*, AN UNAPOLOGETICALLY CHUBBY SHOT, AND (7) THE INSUFFERABLE *PORKER*.

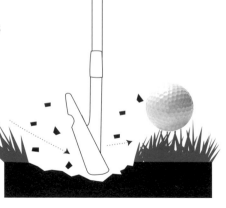

(1) THE LIZ TAYLOR

FAT SHOTS ARE ACHIEVED BY HITTING THE GROUND BEFORE MAKING CONTACT WITH THE BALL. IN SUCH CASES, SHORT ARMS ARE AN ADVANTAGE.

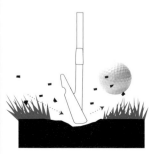

(2) THE STUB

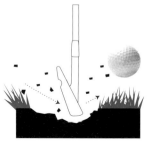

(3) THE CHUNK

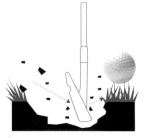

(4) THE CHILI DIP

(5) THE FRITO LAY

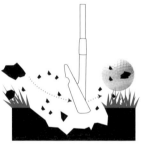

(6) THE ROSEANNE

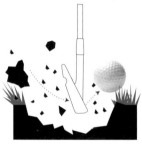

(7) THE PORKER

flub: A sort of weak and fat chip. (See *Fat Shots* box, page 38.)

fluff (to): In the rough, when the club face passes under the ball without making solid contact. As in: "Knee-high in the lettuce, Greg *fluffed* the ball three times before whiffing it."

fluffy lie: A deceptive lie where the ball sits high on top of thick grass.

fluffy (the): The fairway. As in: "It took Hilda an air ball, two flares, and a chunky before she got her ball out on the *fluffy*."

flush: When used as an adjective, it indicates the type of desirable shot where the club face makes solid contact with the ball, but without touching the ground. Sometimes it is used as a verb, as in: "After several unsuccessful earlier attempts, Dr. Hillsborough finally *flushed* a beautiful 3-wood at the 155-yard par-3 12th and ended up hitting someone on the 15th tee." (See *airmail.*)

fly (on the): A way to describe the distance a ball travels before it hits the ground and begins to roll. As in: "Dr. Solomon usually hits them 220 yards *on the fly*, and aims at the cart path for added distance."

flypaper: Refers to a slow green. As in: "Geez, the greens at Binkly Municipal Golf Course are like the *flypaper* in the snack bar."

foot mashie: (old-fashioned) Action of kicking the ball out of trouble towards a better lie For example: "Mrs. Muffington's ball was stuck behind the root of an oak tree, and while she was trying to give it the old *foot mashie*, she lost her balance and fell on a rodent."

THE FOOT-MASHIE OR
THE FOOT WEDGE

foot wedge: The modern version of the foot mashie. Best club in the bag to speed up play.

foozle: An old-fashioned term for a poorly struck shot in which the ball trickles only a few miserable yards forward. (See *Rocca.*)

Fore!: Last word heard before getting beaned. (See *beaned.*)

fountain ball: Another colorful term for a vertical drive. (See *Ascending Tee Shots* diagram, page 40.)

404 (pronounced four-o-four): Derived from the internet, it refers to a ball that can't be found, as in: "404 site not found."

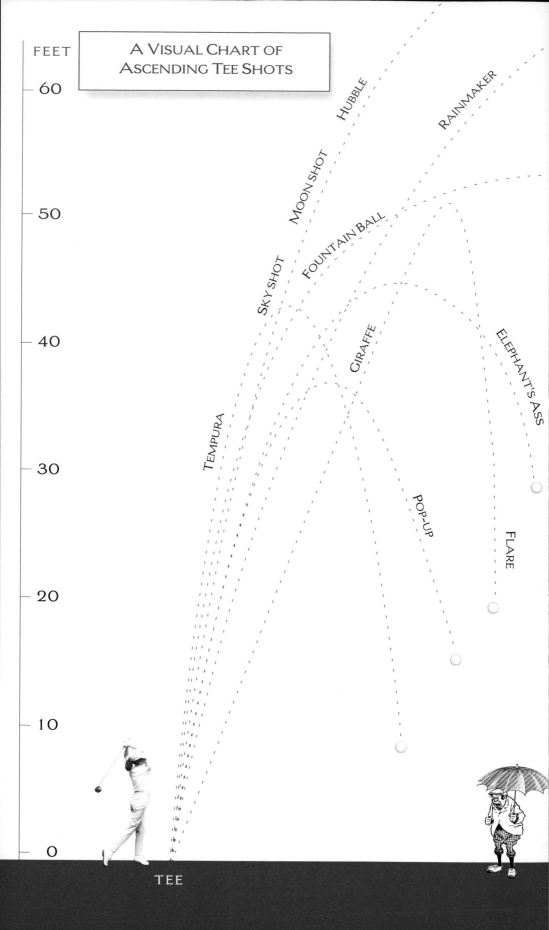

fried egg: A ball half-buried in a bunker. As in: "The 3rd hole had Frank for breakfast today. After taking a bacon strip with his wedge, he ended up with a fried egg in the bunker. He barely got out with his spatula, but then he had a couple of Frito-Lays before getting onto the green."

fringe: The short grass area immediately surrounding the green. See brillo, froghair.

Frisbee: A low-flying shot, just above head-high.

Frisco: A steep downhill putt, as in San Francisco.

Frito-Lay: A fat chip. (See *Fat Shots* diagram, page 38.)

frog eyes: A score of 88. Also called double dogballs or a double snowman.

froghair: The short grass around the green. Known also as apron, brillo, or skirt.

front (the): Short for front nine. "Out" in U.K. golf.

Frosty: The Snowman. A score of 8.

frozen rope: Borrowed from baseball slang. A hard, straight drive.

fudge factor: The difference between the number of strokes actually taken on the course and that which is recorded on the scorecard. As in: "Not counting the *fudge factor*, Herb scored a 115." (Also see *barber, equalizer*.)

full-flaps: Piloting instruction given to the ball to make it land on the green and stop. (Also see *get down* and *sit*.)

fungo: A practice shot. As in: "I'm in trouble now! I spent the whole afternoon hitting *fungoes* and forgot to buy my wife that new garbage compactor she wanted for her birthday."

furniture: The woods. As in: "Mrs. Smillibilick does not carry any irons in her bag. She hits the *furniture* on every shot."(Also see *lumber*.)

ZEPPLIN

gas: The amount of energy imparted to a putt, as in: "George' s putt had too much *gas* and ended up hitting his own bag, costing him the hole and the match."

german: A score of nein.

Geronimo!: A childish but amusing thing to yell when your opponent's *skyball* is about to splash into a water hazard.

get away (to): Refers to a ball getting out of control. As in: "Bob's drive at the 18th *got away* from him, he ended up airmailing the 18th green and he finished with a Bo Derek."

get down: What good players yell to their ball after hitting a short iron to the green.

get Legs: An exhortation used to help the ball fly over a water hazard or roll to the hole.

get up: What most players yell to their ball after hitting a drive, long iron or short iron.

gimme: A putt short enough to be conceded. For example: "When playing for money, Mrs. Neidermeier always asks for some generous *gimmes*."

giraffe: An excessively high drive that reaches for the trees. (See *Ascending Tee Shots* diagram, page 40.)

girlish: An adjective for a putt that stops short of the hole. Not very P.C.

DR. SNODMEISTER'S GIRLISH PUTT
BECOMES A GIMMEE.

give, give: A situation where two players give each other their putts.

going to school: To learn the slope and the speed of a green from someone with a putt similar to yours. For example: "George *went to school* on Phil and still missed his putt by three feet."

golden ferret: A chip-in from the sand.

golfdom: Heavenly residence of the golf gods, living or departed. Local address: World Golf Hall of Fame, Jupiter, Fla.

golf stick: A score of 7.

golf princess: A woman whose outfit and equipment are disproportionately costly compared to her scores, as in: "Beatrice is such a *golf princess*. She's got a brand new titanium driver but she still can't buy a putt."

gonzo: A familiar way of indicating that a ball has gone into the jungle or out of bounds. As in: "After hitting his third O.B. of the day, Nick warned Bernie to stop saying *gonzo*, or Nick would wrap his driver around Bernie's neck. (See *au revoir, bye bye, 404, sayonara.*)

goose pâté: Greenish animal waste found near water hazards. Although it may be deemed a movable impediment, who would want to?

gopher-killer: A drive that flies about six inches above the ground (See *Low Shots* diagram, page92.)

Gordie: A score of 9, hockey Hall of Famer Gordie Howe's number.

gorse: Thick grass found in Scottish rough. Pronounced *gorrrse.*

graphite shaft: The golf pencil. Fastest, cheapest, and surest piece of equipment to improve your score.

grass-cutter: Another member of the ground-hugging family of golf shots. (See *Low Shots* diagram, page 92.)

GORSE

greenie (a): Small bet won by hitting the closest shot to the hole on a par-3.

green light lie: When the ball sits up nicely in the rough, allowing the player to go for the green. As in: "After driving deep into the mahoofka, Fred discovered that he had a *green-light lie* and decided to go for it with his driver. He ended up carding double candles on the hole."

green-stalker: A ball lying behind a tree, near the green. As in: "Bruce's attempt at chipping his *green-stalker* turned into tragedy after the ball ricocheted off a tree and hit him in the nose."

Gretzky. A score of 99

grinder: A player who keeps fighting and does not give up.

grip: Pro slang for backspin.

grip job: A putt that stops within a grip length of the cup. (See *leather*.)

groove (in the): When a golfer's swing follows a successful and reliable pattern. Golf swings don't tend to stay *in the groove* for more than a few days in a row. A few weeks at the most. (Also see *leaking oil, wheels*.)

ground-breaking ceremony: When a player chunks his or her drive on the 1st tee. As in: "Mr. Fromholzer held a *ground-breaking ceremony* last Saturday on the 1st tee at Winged Foot."

Gumbled (to get): To get prematurely praised for a shot, then see the ball miss its target. Named for TV commentator Bryant Gumble, known for his occasional lack of golf judgment.

gust of gravity: The sudden effect of one of nature's fundamental forces on a golf shot. As in: "Georgette's approach had almost cleared the pond when her ball was brought down by a sudden *gust of gravity*."

gutter ball: A skulled drive that starts over the fairway then rolls into the rough.

gut truck: The refreshment cart that delivers the *swing oil*. Also known as a chuck wagon.(See also *quench wench, aiming fluid*.)

GROUND-BREAKING CEREMONY

hacker: The most common type of golfer. What hackers lack in skill they make up in persistence. Also known as a chop, duffer, dub, or mudder.

ham-and-egging: When golf partners balance each other out, alternating between good and bad play. As in: "John and Herb were *ham-and-egging* all through the front nine, but they had an argument at the 10th and John wrapped Herb's driver around a tree."

hand mashie: Shot they used to play before Gene Sarazaen invented the sand wedge in 1930. (See *hand wedge*, below)

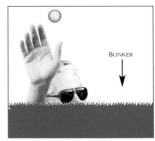

HAND WEDGE

hand wedge: Modern version of the hand mashie. The surest way to get out of a bunker ever since 1930.

hang time: The number of seconds a golf ball stays in the air between the time it leaves the club face and the moment it crashes in the jungle. Worm-burners have no measurable *hang time*.

hanging lie: If the ball lies above the player's feet, it's known as a *hanging lie* or *hanger*. In theory, you're supposed to adjust your aim to the right since the ball will fly left from a *hanger*. In reality, you need not worry since you'll probably chunk it anyway.

happy (a): A great drive, as in: "Clark finally hit a *happy* on 18 after an exhausting round of military golf."

HITTING A HAPPY

hardpan lie: A difficult lie made of compacted dirt such as that found on a road or a muni course in Kansas. (Also see *bare lie, naked lie, Willie ball.*)

harvesting: The practice (outlawed by the USGA) of clearing the rough around your ball with your feet or club.

hat hair: The official stick-to-the-forehead summer hairstyle of tour pros at postround interviews.

Heads up!: A friendly warning to players ahead of you, just in case you don't whiff the ball.

heely: Also known as a heeler, an unsettling type of wood shot where the ball connects with the heel of the club, sending it off in a semi-lateral direction. (See *Oral Roberts.*)

Helen Keller: A blind shot.

HARDPAN LIE

heliputter: A low-flying type of aircraft sometimes seen hovering above the green after a short-tempered player misses a putt. Dangerous and disgraceful.

herding: When the entire foursome walks to each ball, perhaps to give advice or lend support. Extremely annoying when you're in the foursome behind them.

hickories: Old-fashioned word for golf clubs. As in: "Say there, Alphonse, do I see a new set of *hickories* in your rumble seat?"

hit a barn: Exhortation addressed at a ball in flight, hoping for a lucky bounce back into the fairway. Also referred to as "Hit a house!"

Hitler: A ball that never made it out of the bunker.

Hoffa: A ball that is never seen again. (See *gonzo, 404*)

Hollywood handicap: An artificially low handicap obtained by returning only your best scores. Looks nice on paper but can get costly.

home: The second nine holes on a course, also known as the back nine.

home hole: The 18th hole.

home run: A long, beautiful winning drive. Can also be used to describe a shot that is hit over the fence and, thus, out-of-bounds.

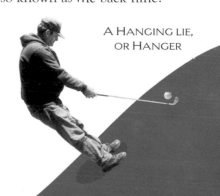

A HANGING LIE, OR HANGER

homesick gopher: A fast putt that hits the hole and scurries in.

honors: When golf was still a gentleman's game, the lowest scorer on a hole was given the *honor* of teeing off first on the next hole. In modern golf, the *honors* are often not honored. (See *ready golf*.)

hood the club face: To grip the club as to close the face and promote a low, right to left ball trajectory.

Hoover: A sweeping hook that gets sucked into the woods.

horseshoe it: When a putt does 180 degrees around the rim of the hole. (Also see *paint job*.)

hospital zone: The place to go to fix your swing, or the practice area. Also called Murderer's Row, rockpile. (See *beat balls, break some eggs*.)

hot: Low-trajectory shot with no backspin. As in: "Joe's ball came out *hot* off the rough, buzzed the green and broke Mr. Luddington's kneecap."

hubble: A drive that goes so high it can see the stars. (See *Ascending Tee Shots* diagram, page 40.)

hummer: A golf cart. (Also see *BIPmobile*.)

hunt (in the): Pro-tour talk for a player who still has a chance to win nearing the end of a tournament. As in: "To the surprise of many, Mrs. Plushbottom was once again *in the hunt* going into the playoff at the Senior Ladies' Open."

ice rink: A description applied to a very fast green, usually after a putt has rolled a considerable distance past the hole. (Also see *bikini wax.*)

iffy lie: A lie that leaves the player in doubt as to the outcome of the shot. As in: "Facing an *iffy lie* from the rough, Mr. Griffin pulled out the old 7-wood and executed a perfect airball."

inside: When your opponent's ball lands close to the hole, but yours ends up closer, you are said to be *inside*. (Also see *away, USA.*)

Irish birdie: A birdie scored after hitting a mulligan.

THE LIES OF GOLF

Of all the lies known to golfers, the green light lie (1) might well be the most dangerous. The temptation to pull out the furniture is great. A comfortable cushion of grass under the ball makes the fluffy lie (2) a favorite among the ladies. Men pretend to hate it because of the flyers, but that's another lie. The iffy lie (3) is just that: iffy. You just don't know how the shot is going to come off. The hanger (4) comes with a 90% chance of hitting it fat. Choke down on the shaft or better, give it the old foot-wedge. While in the sand, the buried lie (5) requires a minimum of two strokes, usually more. Think hand-wedge. The fried egg (6) looks easy enough, but watch out for Vin Skully. With a naked lie (7) better stick to the putter, and for the hardpan (8), check the local rules, then take a free drop.

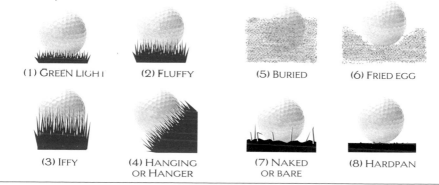

(1) GREEN LIGHT   (2) FLUFFY   (5) BURIED   (6) FRIED EGG

(3) IFFY   (4) HANGING OR HANGER   (7) NAKED OR BARE   (8) HARDPAN

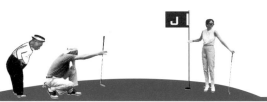

jab: To hit a quick, wristy and ill-fated putting stroke.

jack it up (to): 1) To tee up the ball. As in: "*Jack it up*, Birdie Boy!" 2) To improve one's lie. As in: "The ball that Leon *jacked up* in the rough turned out to be mine."

jail (to be in or to get out of): To be in the woods or to get out of the woods. For example: "Dave tried to get out of *jail* with his four-iron, but his ball disappeared in the branches of a tree and never came back down." (See *backpacking*, *nature walk*, *tree iron*.)

jamalies: Resort golfers with a bad swing and an attitude to match. (Also see *jerk*.)

jam in: To make an aggressive putt. As in: "Lucy was on the green in 7, but she *jammed in* a 3-footer to win the club championship."

JAIL

jamoke: King of all jamalies.

jar: The hole. (Also see *barrel*, *can*, *cup*, *tin*.) Can also be used as a verb, meaning to hole a putt. As in: "Carston Valentine, who was putting for a new Mercedes, studied the break for five minutes in an attempt to *jar* his 10-footer."

jerk: To strike a putt with a wristy, off-line stroke. As in: "Carston Valentine *jerked* his 10-footer and had to drive home in his Ford Pinto." Can also be used as a noun.

Jesus: A shot that walks across water. (Also see *skid shot.*)

John Birch: A shot that is way to the right.

Johnny Cochran: To face a shot with such a terrible lie that only *Johnny Cochran* can save you.

jug: The hole. As in "Brad is an aggressive player. He always goes for the *jug.*"

juice: 1) Golf lingo for backspin; 2) The forward energy of a ball in motion. For example: "Richie's putt was right on line, but it had too much *juice* and rolled past the hole and into the lake." 3) Nickname of a famous hacker saved by *Johnny Cochran.*

juicy lie: A lie in which the ball is sitting up, also known as a green light lie.

jump: What the ball often does when hit from the tall grass. Due to complex technical factors, it comes out too strong and usually rolls straight into the bunker across the green.

jungle: Dense, wooded rough.

jungle book: The schematic course guidebook. As in: "The *jungle book* at Pebble costs more than the greens fees at Binkly Links."

junk: Any sort of small prize money at stake on a hole. (Also see *candy.*)

junk man: Someone who likes to play for small, side bets. (See *junk.*)

JESUS

keg man: The guy in the foursome who will pay for the beer. As in: "Jimbo was the *keg man* right from the 1st hole, and never relinquished his position."

Kevorkian: A killer swing or a suicidal shot. As in: "Bubba announced he was gonna hit a *Kevorkian* at the 445-yard, dog leg 9th, but he got in trouble and ended up in jail."

kick: The bounce of the ball after hitting the ground. Bad *kicks* outnumber good *kicks* 10-to-1.

kick-in distance: A technical term describing a short distance between the ball and the hole. (See *Putt Measurements* diagram on opposite page.)

kill: To put all of one's strength into a drive. Although *killing* sometimes results in a happy, it is more often the cause of golfing woes, including topping, skulling, duck hooks, Roseannes, chili dipping, rainmakers, power fades, and slooks. The 1st Commandment of Golf: "Thou Shalt Not *Kill* the Ball." (See *Kevorkian*.)

klingons: Particles of dirt that remain attached to the blade after taking a divot.

knee-knocker: A treacherous short putt. As in: "In his early days, Arnie made a lot of *knee-knockers*."

KNEE KNOCKER

knife: To skull and slice the ball at the same time. Also, another name for the one-iron. But no one can hit a one-iron anyway.

knock it in: To make a putt. As in: "John knocked out his opponent by *knocking in* a 40-footer."

knockdown shot: A shot with an intentionally low trajectory. As in: "With his fondness for *knockdown shots*, it was only a matter of time before Carl knocked somebody out." (See *punch shot*.)

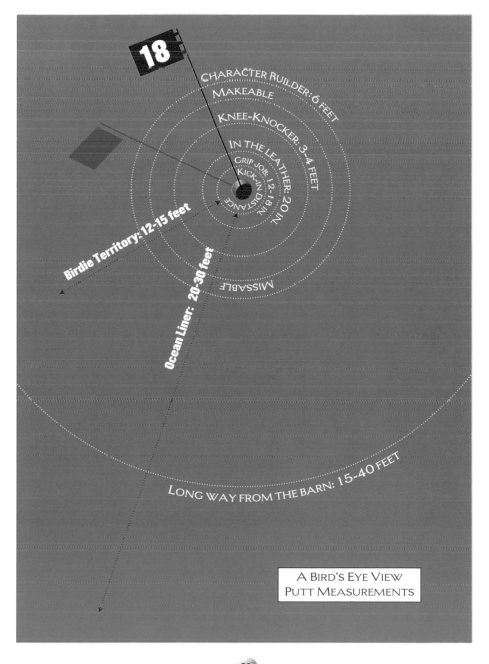

CHARACTER BUILDER: 6 FEET
MAKEABLE
KNEE-KNOCKER: 3-4 FEET
IN THE LEATHER: 20 FEET
GRIP JOB: 12-18 IN.
KICK-IN DISTANCE
Birdie Territory: 12-15 feet
Ocean Liner: 20-30 feet
MISSABLE
LONG WAY FROM THE BARN: 15-40 FEET

A BIRD'S EYE VIEW
PUTT MEASUREMENTS

LAUNCHING A LATERAL ON A LASSIE

lag: To hit a long putt softly, so that the ball will come to a stop at or near the hole.

landscaping: To improve one's lie, especially in the rough. *Landscaping* is a gross violation of the rules.

lassie: A dogleg to the left.

lateral: A golf shot that takes off at a sharp side-angle. As in: "During the club championship, Mrs. Kerrigan hit a *lateral* off the 1st tee and she insisted they remove the starter's hut for her to play her second."

launch: To hit a long, powerful, high-trajectory drive. (See *scud*.)

Laurel and Hardy: A score of 10. Also known as Bo Derek.

law dog: The course ranger. As in: "When asked what they wanted to do after retirement, most men interviewed in Minnesota declared that they wanted to be *law dogs* in Florida."

lawn darts: A derogatory name for the Royal and Ancient game.

Lawrence of Arabia: A player who spends a lot of time in the sand.

lawyer (golf): A person intent on ruining everyone else's day by insisting on a strict respect of the rules. As in: "Dave is just a *golf lawyer*. He wanted to give Bernie a two-stroke penalty for failing to report my foot mashie."

GOLF LAWYER

Lawrence of Arabia: A player who spends a lot of time in the sand.

lay up: To play safely short of a water hazard. As in: "Bob wisely decided to *lay up* short of the lake with a five-iron. It's too bad he couldn't tell the water was only 125 yards away."

leak: A shot that takes off straight but then drifts off to the right. (Lefthanded golfers *leak* to the left.)

leaking oil: Automotive expression indicating that a player's game or score is steadily deteriorating. As in: "Eugene the Machine had a great front nine, but he was so hot he finally blew a gasket and *leaked oil* until he ripped up his scorecard and went BIPSIC on the 17th green."

leather: The grip of the club.

leather (inside the): Using the putter as a measuring stick, a ball lying between the blade and the start of the grip is said to be *inside the leather* and usually a gimme.

legs: What players want golf balls to get as they are traveling toward the hole.

lettuce: The tall rough. As in: "Arthur's game was off and he spent most of the day in the *lettuce*." (Also see *mahoofka*, *spinach*.)

licorice stick: A graphite shaft.

Linda Ronstadt: A drive that overshoots your opponent's. As in: "Hey, Nick!" Bernie yelled, "that was a *Linda Ronstadt*! I just blew by you!" A reference to "Blue Bayou," a song Ronstadt made popular. It's not a good idea to use this one more than once during a round.

lint: The fringe around the green. (Also see *apron*, *brillo*, *froghair*, *skirt*.)

lip out: A putt that kisses the rim of the hole but chooses not to go in. (See *Putt Measurement* diagram, page 53.)

liprosy: A frightening disease that afflicts millions of weekend golfers, the symptom being putts that keep skimming the lip of the hole but refusing to drop in. Although some seek treatment in the emergency room, there is no known cure.

LEON HITS A LINDA RONSTADT

Liz Taylor: A shot that is a little fat, but still beautiful. (See *Fat Shots* diagram, page 38.)

loaf: A large, meaty divot. (See *The Dirt on Divots* diagram, page 32.)

lobster: The lob wedge. As in: "To get out of the lettuce, Barton wisely chose the *lobster*."

logging: Chopping a ball out of an ancient growth. (Also see *jail, lumberyard*.)

long ball: To hit the *long ball* is a cherished dream of all golfers.

Long-Eared Society: A McCordism for the Master's Tournament Committee.

long way from the barn (to be): The position of facing a very long putt.

LOGGING

loop: Eighteen holes. As in: "Every Sunday, Randy and Greg go for a quick *loop* before church."

looper: A caddie. Also known as a bag rat, bird dog, double looper, or flag waver.

Lorena Bobbit: A nasty slice.

lot (to be all over the): To spray one's shots in all directions.

lumber: The driver. As in: "Ruppert's decision to hit the lumber at 13 turned out to be ill-fated." Also called big dog or chief.

Lumber City: A long course, requiring extensive use of the woods. See *The World of Golf* diagram, page 35.)

lumberyard: The trees. As in: "Jerry was wearing his favorite plaid shirt when he sliced a five-wood into the *lumberyard*."

MAKEABLE / MISSABLE

mahoofka: A vicious type of rough with knee-high, thick, tangly grass. Especially developed by the CIA's secret weed laboratory under contract from the USGA.

makeable: Any putt that you think you can make. Putts from three to 30 feet in length can be labeled as *makeable*, depending on a golfer's skill level and degree of foolishness.

mallard: A duck hook.

manicured: The state of a perfectly maintained course or green.

marble: A golf ball.

Mario Andretti: A drive that hits the cart path and keeps rolling and rolling. As in: "Since Uncle Fred has discovered the *Mario Andretti*, he has shaved seven strokes off his handicap." (See *cart-path management, member's bounce, willie.*)

Marquis de Sod: The greenkeeper responsible for painful pin placements. (The original *Marquis de Sod* was the inventor of Golf Architorture.)

Marshall Dillon: The course ranger.

marshmallow: Pro slang for a worn-out, out-of-round Balata ball.

Marv Albert: An approach shot with a lot of bite.

mast: The flagstick. (Also see *pin*.)

meat (left on that bone): A statement describing a putt that stops significantly short of the hole, as in: "Hey Barry, there's a lot of *meat left on that bone*."

Meat-and-potatoes par-4: A long, straight par 4 without the fairway bunkers, menacing rough, or water hazards that would make for a more exotic meal.

member's bounce: A lucky bounce of the ball, indicating that the player knows the course well and where to make the ball bounce. A 1960s type expression.

merde: A curse word liberally used while playing le golf.

Mickey Mouse: Derogatory adjective for a golf course with controversial design features. As in: "The greens on Pinehurst No. 2 are just too *Mickey Mouse* for me."

Mick Jagger: A putt that lips out of the hole.

mile: The distance pros and very good golfers are said to hit their drives. In actual fact, the longest drive on record is only .26th of a mile, but to exclaim: "Hot dogies! He hit that thing .26th of a mile!" has little impact and is probably why it was never adopted.

military golf: Same as army golf, i.e., left, right, left, right. (Also see *Z golf*, *Zorro*.)

missable: A putt that can be missed, i.e., in the eyes of one's opponent, any putt longer than a tap-in. (See *Putt Measurement* box page 53.)

BEATING BALLS ON MURDERERS' ROW

moonshot: A high-flying tee shot. (See *Ascending Tee Shots* diagram, page 40.)

moonwalking: Ball with a lot of backspin, walking backwards on the green.

mop squeezer: A slow player. As in: "We were rushing to get in nine holes before dark, but ran into a bunch of *mop squeezers.*"

Morgan Fairchild: McCordism for a nice-looking shot, a little thin, but pretty.

Moses: A ball rescued from the water (Also see *stogie soaker, water wedge.*)

moving day: Saturday: The day a pro who missed the cut gets on the road for the next tournament. Can be Friday night, too. (See *trunk-slammer.*)

Mrs. Doubtfire: Someone who spends too much time in a dress.

mudder: Old-fashioned slang for a bad golfer. (Also see *dub.*)

muerto: Dead in Spanish. (Also see *dead.*)

mulligan: A penalty-free chance at a second tee shot. Dispense freely when playing with your boss. (Also see *culligan, shapiro.*)

mully: A mulligan in common terms.

muni: A municipal golf course.

murderers' row: The driving range. As in: "I was so upset with my game that I spent the whole afternoon on *murderer's row.*" (Also see *rockpile.*)

A WALLBANGER

nail (to): To hit a powerful and accurate golf shot. For example: "Herb *nailed* his drive on the dogleg 10th, and his ball vanished into the jungle."

naked lie: A grassless lie, as in: "Lady Plushbottom found her ball resting on a *naked lie* and used the old foot-wedge to get it out onto the fluffy." See *The Lies of Golf* diagram, page 49. (Also see *bare lie, hardpan*.)

nassau: A popular form of betting on a golf game which involves three wagers of equal amounts on the front nine, the back nine, and the total score. As in: "Bob and Bing like to play for $2.00 *nassaus*." See *The World of Golf*, page 35.

nature boy/girl: A golfer who spends a lot of time enjoying the woods (as in trees).

AUNT BETTY TAKES A
NATURE WALK

NATURE GIRL

nature walk: A round of golf spent mostly in the mahoofka.

nestle it: To hit an approach shot very close to the hole. Same as snuggling, cozy it.

nickel: A score of five. Also, another name for the five-iron.

19th hole: Generally refers to the bar in the clubhouse. A few courses have genuine par-3 *19th holes* used for playoffs, so their clubhouse bars must be called the 20th hole.

nip: To hit a wedge shot with a shallow divot, imparting a lot of backspin to the ball. For example: "Mrs. McFadden tried to *nip* her ball over the bunker, but she skulled it instead and she ended up facing Yasir Arafat."

NITBY. Acronym for Not In The Bunker Yet

NITWY: Acronym for Not In The Water Yet. As in: "Jimbo is NITBY, the Donmeister is NITWY, and I'm BIPSIC."

noodle: To hit a curving ball. (Also see *banana ball*.)

North Carolina: N.C., or no scorecard returned.

nuke: War-related terminology. To *nuke* the ball is to hit it very hard and long. (Also see *bomb, cream, crunch, F-14, kill, smoke*.)

NATURE BOY
DENIED PAROLE

O.B.: Out of bounds. The two most hated letters in golf. (Also see *Oscar Brown, O'Brien*)

O'Brien: See above.

ocean liner: A putt that sails across the green ocean.

Oh boy: Out-of-Bounds.

Oldsmobile scramble: A ball that flies into the parking lot. As in: "Chester is playing in the Oldsmobile Scramble again this week."

one time: A desperate plea addressed to a putt nearing the hole, especially in the wake of several paint jobs, rim burners and trips across the cellophane bridge.

Oprah golf: One thin shot, one fat shot, thin, fat, thin, fat, and so on and so forth.

Oral Roberts: A shot that is hit with the heel of the club, the term is a secondary spin off from the concept of heeler. *Oral Roberts* was a healer. It's best not to do this.

Oscar Brown: 1960s tour slang for out-of-bounds. (Also see *O.B., O'Brien.*)

Oscar Bravo: Out-of-bounds. Again. (Also see *O.B., O'Brien, oh boy, Oscar Brown.*)

over clubbing: Selecting a club longer than needed for a specific shot.

over cooked: A shot or putt with too much power. (Also see *airmail.*)

pace: A technical term for the speed of a putt. Can also be used to describe the speed of play. As in: "Excuse me, Mr. and Mrs. Crosby, I hate to have to tell you, but there are three holes open ahead of you and you'll have to pick up the pace." (Also see *foot wedge, mop squeezer, pick up, snail trail.*)

PAINT JOB

paint job: A putt that paints the inside of the hole and then rolls out.

Pamela Anderson (looking for): Spending a lot of time on the beach. As in: "After a morning of Oprah golf, Tom went *looking for Pamela Anderson* on the last six holes." (See *beach.*)

pancake: Another term for a flop shot.

par-2 course: The practice green. Where the Boss of the Moss rules.

PBS: Acronym for Post Birdie Syndrome. A common affliction. (Also see *ABFU, ABSU.*)

peg: A tee.

pegboard: A recently aerated green. As in: "We drove 100 miles and paid 55 bucks a pop to putt on *pegboard* greens!"

pen pal: Pencil. (Also see *equalizer, graphite shaft.*)

persimmon (to put on): To hit the driver, in reference to when the woods were actually made of wood. (Also see *chief, lumber.*)

	REVENGE	BERT'S FOLLY	SKULL & BONES	CULLIGAN'S ALLEY	SAYONARA!	BUNKER'S TRUST	NO-SEE-UMS	SING-SING	HOME ALONE	BINKLY LINKS COUNTRY CLUB	IN	TOTAL	HDCP	NET
	10	11	12	13	14	15	16	17	18		IN	TOTAL	HDCP	NET
	613	456	447	386	439	206	521	188	443		3699	7252		
	569	433	417	370	423	201	509	177	413		3512	6869		
	461	388	350	355	411	189	456	159	380		3149	6337		
	425	358	335	323	393	154	405	143	352		2888	5825		
	5	4	4	4	4	3	5	3	4		36	72		
	5	3	7	5	5	1	5	3	8		42	88		
	5	4	4	3	9	3	6	6	6		46	106		
	5	4	3	4	3	3	5	3	3		33	66		
	11	4	3	5	4	5	10	3	5		45	88		
	5	4	4	4	5	3	5	3	4		37			
	2	10	12	14	6	16	4	18	8					

PHILIPS PETROLEUM AND PIANO KEYS

Philips Petroleum: A score of 66. (Also see *Route*.)

piano keys: A score of 88.

pick up (to): Commendable but all too rare show of consideration for the others players in your foursome and on the golf course. (Also see *BIPSIC, pocketized*.)

pick-up truck: Where you keep the wrenches. (Also see *BIPmobile, hummer*.)

pigeon: A golfer with a big ego whose wallet is the target of better players. In his early days as a pro, Sam Snead was a skilled pigeon-hunter.

pill: The golf ball, in the days of Walter Hagen.

pin (the): The flagstick.

pinch the ball (to): To squeeze the ball between the club face and the turf when hitting with an iron. Alleged to produce backspin. (See *action*.)

pipe (right down the): Right in the middle of the fairway. For example: "Laverne smacked a 20-yard worm-burner right down the *pipe*."

pitching wood: Club used to hit a short, more or less vertical wood shot from either the tee or the fairway. The *pitching wood* always delivers an unpleasant surprise. (See *Ascending Tee Shots* diagram, page 40.)

A POP-UP SHOT MADE WITH A PITCHING WOOD

pizza ball (a): A slice. As in: "Uncle Vito hits a lot of *pizza balls*."

plates: Another words for tee markers. (See *blues, tips, tiger tees*.)

played darts: Balls already on the green.

plumb bobbing: A professional green-reading technique where the player dangles the putter in front of his nose, closes one eye and finally asks his caddie which way the ball is going to go. (See *break*.)

plumber: Someone who drains a lot of putts.

pocketized: A ball which rests in the pocket is termed pocketized. Usually the result of a recent negative golf experience.

poke (a): Action of striking the ball. As in: "Give it a good *poke*, Bertha!"

poley (to make a): Sinking a putt within a flagstick length of the hole. May be worth a buck or a quarter, depending what kind of company you keep.

pool shark: A so-so golfer from tee to green, but fearsome once on the dance-floor.

popcorn shot: Another high tee shot. (See *Ascending Tee Shots* diagram, page 40.)

pop-up shot: A drive or fairway wood that travels more or less vertically. Often achieved with the pitching wood or the wedge wood. (See *Ascending Tee Shots* diagram, page 40.)

porker: The fattest of the fat shots. (See *Fat Shots* diagram, page 38.)

postage stamp: A small green. As in "Bernie 'The Mailman' Doyle airmailed the *postage stamp*."

potato masher: A flat-headed putter. As in: "Mr. Stefanos pulled out the old *potato masher* and drained a 60-footer."

THE PLUMBER

power blade: An awesome skull.

power fade: An awesome slice.

pre mix: Hard sand in a bunker that has the consistency of concrete.

press: A term for a new bet or game within an existing match.

pro side (the): The opposite of the amateur side.

provisional: A second ball hit from the tee, on the chance that the first one is lost. As in: "Mrs. Maladroit has the irritating habit of hitting a *provisional* on almost every hole."

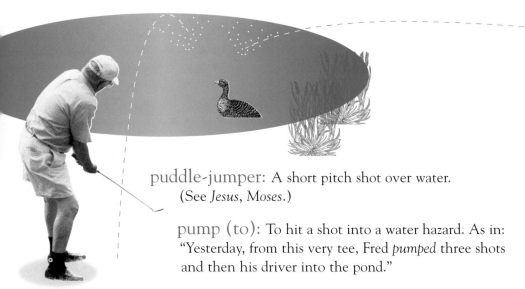

puddle-jumper: A short pitch shot over water. (See *Jesus, Moses.*)

pump (to): To hit a shot into a water hazard. As in: "Yesterday, from this very tee, Fred *pumped* three shots and then his driver into the pond."

TO PUMP

pumped-up: Glandular reaction following a series of good shots. (See *adrenaline, ABSU, airmail, Cadillac Strut, overcooked.*)

punch shot: A low-iron shot played against the wind. A semi-skulled wedge shot can often be covered up by calling it a *punch shot.*

pure: Adverb to describe a perfect golf shot. As in: "The best shot of my life was on this hole when I hit a six-iron so *pure*, it brought tears to my eyes. That was in 1977."

putting jessie: An excellent putter. (Also see *plumber.*)

quacker: A duck hook. (Also see *mallard.*)

quail high: A shot three feet higher than a bug cutter. (See *Low Trajectory Shots* diagram, page 92.)

quench wench: The young lady who drives the refreshment cart.

quitting: 1) Failure to complete a full swing after hitting the ball, often resulting in a skull or slice; 2) Failure to complete a full round, often resulting in temporary banishment from a regular foursome.

quiver: Term for a golf bag. As in: "Robin had more clubs than shots in her *quiver.*"

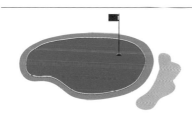

rabbit: A golfer who scrambles from furrow to furrow.

rag: The flag.

radio station: A score in the 100s, like KGOLF 105.

rainmaker: A cloud-piercing shot. (See *Ascending Tee Shots* diagram, page 40.)

rake it in: To pick up one's ball.

ram (to): To hole a putt with an aggressive stroke. At a minimum, the ball should hit the back of the cup before going in. As in: "Marla *rammed* one in at the 18th to win the club championship with a smoking score of 118."

rap (a): A solid strike with the putter. Giving a putt a good *rap* may send the ball into the hole or dramatically increase your chance of three-putting. (See *zap*.)

rattle-in (to): Sound made by the ball after falling into the cup.

razor blade (the): The one-iron.

ready golf: Style of play generally encountered on public courses. Whoever is not washing his balls, recounting his previous hole's score, firing up a cigar or taking a sip of his Budweiser gets to tee-off first. (See *honors*.)

real estate: The distance remaining between the ball and the hole, especially if vast. Can also be used in the phrase they showed us all the *real estate*, meaning the blue tees were set as far back as they go. (Also see *meat*.)

recovery room: The bar. (Also see *19th hole*.)

Red Grange: A score of 77.

regulation: To reach the dance-floor with one shot on a par-3, 2 shots on a par-4, and three on a par-5.

release: Order or imploration addressed at the ball to make it roll further after hitting the green. Not necessary at the British Open.

reload: To tee-up a new ball after hitting the previous one in the water or out of bounds. As in: "During the third round of the 1984 Masters, Tom had to *reload* six times before hitting the 12th green."

rescue operation: When an entire foursome is looking for a lost ball. (See *herding, roadblock, snail trail*.)

rim burner: A putt that rolls over the edge of the hole, but refuses to go in.

rip it (to): What may happen after you grip it.

roadblock (a): The foursome just ahead. One of the most dreaded hazards on a golf course. (See *herding, mop squeezer, rescue operation, snail trail*.)

ROB: Acronym for Ran Out of Balls. (See *six-ball course*.)

robbed (to get): How one feels when a putt that should absolutely, positively, legitimately go in, does not.

RoboDriver (a): A metal driver with a big head. As in: "The head of Dan's new *RoboDriver* is bigger than his."

Rocca: An exceptional combination of a chili-dip, followed by an ocean liner, first demonstrated by Costantino Rocca during the last round of the British Open in 1995.

rock (a): A hardcover, 100 compression, golf ball at 7:30 a.m.

Rockefeller (a): A chip or putt that ends up dead in the hole.

Rock Hudson: A putt that looks straight but is not. (See *Putting Measurement* diagram, page 53.)

rock pile (the): The driving range. As in: "Mrs. Worthington spent the afternoon on the *rock pile*, hitting the furniture."

rollercoaster: A round of golf with a sickening pattern of high and lows. Also used to describe a hilly golf course.

Rommel (a): Taking several strokes to get out of the sand. As in: "Monty had a *Rommel* at the Morroco Open."

roodle (a): In match play, a player who does not win a single hole. As in: "After last Saturday's round, Jimbo was elected to the International *Roodle* Hall of Fame."

Roseanne (a): McCordism for a fat shot. (See *Fat Shots* diagram, page38.)

rough rider (a): A player who spends a lot of time in the rough.

round robin (a): Three-putting from three different sides.

Route (shooting the): A round of 66. As in: "Looks like Jack is going to *shoot the Route* at the Tucson Open this afternoon."

Rover (a): A dogleg to the right.

rug (a): A sizable divot resembling a hairpiece. (See *The Dirt on Divots* diagram, page 32.)

runway: The fairway.

ROCK HUDSON MEETS ROCKEFELLER

RuPaul: Another Gary McCordism. A slice that turns into a hook. May require elective swing surgery.

sack: A golf bag. A golfer who hits the sack with his or her ball incurs a two-stroke penalty or loses the hole.

salvage operation: A foursome searching for a lost ball. (Also see *rescue operation*.)

sandbagger: A greedy person whose game is better than his or her handicap indicates. On the other hand, a *reverse-sandbagger* would rather lose money than show a high handicap.

sandy (to get a): To save par while playing from a bunker.

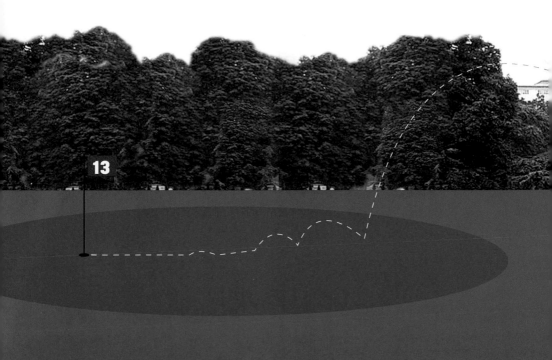

13

sauce: Backspin. (Also see *action*, *juice*.)

Saudi Arabia: A sandy region in *The World of Golf*. (Also see *beach*, *bunker*, *Hitler*.)

sawed-off wedge: A short wedge shot played while choking down on the grip.

sayonara: "Farewell" in Japanese. Delivered just before a ball hits the *misu*.

schwag: Free balls, shirts, and other logo-enhanced corporate gifts bestowed on pro-am participants before they disgrace themselves in public.

scoop (to): To pick the ball cleanly off the ground. Next step up is a skull.

scrape it around: To play a bad round of golf. As in: "I had 52 on the front, 57 on the back. I *scraped it around* all day."

scratch: A zero-handicap golfer. Usually a stockbroker, an independently wealthy person or a club pro. (See *sandbagger*, *sweater-and-shoe pro*.)

screamer: A very powerful drive. As in: "The Vice President's drive at the eighth was a *screamer*. Unfortunately someone should have screamed 'Fore!' after he hit it."

A SHEDDIE

FROM SNOWMEN TO DOGBALLS:
A LOOK AT THE NUMBERS OF GOLF

FROGTOWN MUNICIPAL GOLF LINKS

	MEADOW VISTA	HOMER'S WAY	INTO THE WOODS	GONE FISHIN'	GOD DAMMIT	BEAVER'S LAIR	DUCK HOOK	SHANK-RI-LA	HOT DOG CITY	
	1	2	3	4	5	6	7	8	9	OUT
TIPS	407	450	338	569	485	227	401	490	189	3553
WHITE	396	441	330	499	463	204	391	490	189	3357
MIDDLE	375	411	313	474	485	195	381	490	189	3188
LADIES	359	384	305	446	422	174	312	411	124	2937
MEN'S PAR	4	4	4	5	4	3	4	5	3	36
Bernie	4	4	5	6	5	4	5	6	2	41
Jimbo	8	8	8	11	8	8	8	8	8	60
Nick	5	4	3	4	3	3	5	3	3	33
Heidi	10	5	4	5	4	5	5	5	3	43
LADIES PAR	4	4	4	5	5	3	4	5	3	37
HANDICAP	9	7	13	3	1	15	11	5	17	

Labels: AUDI, BO DEREK, BOGEY TRAIN, DEUCE, DOG BALLS, NICKELS

FROGTOWN MUNICIPAL GOLF LINKS

	REVENGE	BERT'S FOLLY	SKULL & BONES	CULLIGAN'S ALLEY	SAYONARA!	BUNKER'S TRUST	NO-SEE-UMS	SING-SING	HOME ALONE	IN	TOTAL	HDCP	NET
	10	11	12	13	14	15	16	17	18	IN	TOTAL	HDCP	NET
	613	456	447	386	439	206	521	188	443	3699	7252		
	569	433	417	370	423	201	509	177	413	3512	6869		
	461	388	350	355	411	189	456	159	380	3149	6337		
	425	358	335	323	393	154	405	143	352	2888	5825		
	5	4	4	4	4	3	5	3	4	36	72		
	5	3	7	5	5	1	5	3	8	42	83		
	5	4	9	3	9	3	6	6	6	46	106		
	5	4	3	4	3	3	5	3	3	33	66		
	11	4	3	5	4	5	10	3	5	45	88		
	5	4	4	4	5	3	5	3	4	37			
	2	10	12	14	6	16	4	18	8				

Labels: GERMAN, ABSU/ABFU, CANDLES, ACE, SNOWMAN, RADIO STATION, THE ROUTE, DOUBLE DOG BALLS, LAUREL & HARDY

screws (to hit the ball between the): To make solid contact when hitting the driver (i.e., between the screws holding the face plate). This once-popular expression has become obsolete with the advent of metal woods. Fortunately for the game, the drivers may be screwless but not the drivees.

scud: A long, high drive with questionable accuracy. (See *launch*.)

scuff: A miserable putt where the putter head scrapes the turf just before making contact with the ball. Applicable to chip shots as well.

BETWEEN THE SCREWS

sea level: A score of 100.

semi-skull: A shot halfway between a solid shot and a skull. The ball will generally fly low, but the results may be acceptable. (Also see *skank*, *That'll play*.)

serving cake: To keep slicing. As in: "Leon has been *serving cake* all afternoon."

service entrance: The left, right or back side of the hole.

7-up: A score of 79.

shag bag: A bag for carrying practice balls.

shagging: The mundane occupation of picking up practice balls. As in: "I'm afraid Mr. Skullbuddy can't come to the phone right now. He is *shagging* golf balls in the backyard."

shank: The five-letter word of golf.

shapiro: A mulligan at a Jewish club.

sheddie: Making par after the ball has bounced off a shed or any sort of human edifice. (See *condo golf*.)

shoot: To score. As in: "Whadja *shoot* today, Daryl? Double dogballs, as usual?"

shooting gallery: An easy golf course. As in: "Augusta has become a *shooting gallery*. They better put some mahoofka in there."

short game: The part of the game they say you should concentrate on to really improve your score. Fat chance.

short grass: The fairway. (Also see *fluffy*, *runway*.)

short stick: The putter. As in: "Ben is better with the *short stick* than with the lumber." (Also see *broomstick*, *equalizer*, *potato masher*.)

side-door: Same as service entrance.

sink a putt (to): To make a putt, as in: "Barry was out of luck on 18th. He almost *sank* a 30-footer for par, but the ball stopped just short of the hole and he picked up after scuffing his tap-in."

sit: Canine obedience command to make a ball in flight come down, or a rolling putt stop.

sit on it: To put all one's weight into a shot. (Also see *belly snap*, *cheeks*.)

sitting up: Refers to a ball resting on top of the grass, as opposed to being buried in the mahoofka.

six-ball course: A tough course.

size L: A long drive.

skank: In pro talk, a low, sub-optimal shot that still yields acceptable results. A super-shot for you and me. (Also see *semi-skull*.)

skid row: A McCordism for a skid shot.

skid shot: A ball that skims across the surface of a water hazard, only to bury itself in the weeds that line the far bank. (See *Jesus*, *Moses*.)

skin: Hole-by-hole play where a point or *skin* is won by the golfer with the lowest score on a hole. If there is a tie, no *skin* is awarded and the point is carried over to the next hole. In professional golf, a *skins* game can yield some serious candy.

skinny: A thin shot. (See *Morgan Fairchild*.)

skirt: Short grass surrounding the green. Similar to fringe. (Also see *apron*, *brillo*, *collar*.)

skull: To hit the top part of the ball with the bottom edge of the club. Can be used either as a noun or verb, as in: "Johnny *skulled* his 7-iron shot and landed in the bunker, where he hit another *skull* and lost the hole."

skyball: A pop-up drive also known as a rainmaker or flarc. (See *Ascending Tee Shots* diagram, page 40.)

SLICK SLACKS

skywriting: In pro slang, the action of changing swing plane at the top of the backswing. Jim Furyk is a successful *skywriter*.

slam dunk: A fast putt that hits the back of the cup, pops up, and to the great satisfaction of the player, drops in.

slick slacks: Shiny polyester pants favored by pros in the 1970s. Often beltless and flammable, they were available in a variety of terrible colors and patterns.

slider: 1) A delicate side-hill putt, or 2) Golf slacks made of synthetic materials with an adjustable waist.

slook: A slice that turns into a hook. Considered an act of God by most insurance companies.

smile: A wide grin on the face of a golf ball, usually caused by a skull. Except for the balata-covered kind, golf balls aren't *smiling* much nowadays. The advent of cut-proof covers has made them sad.

smiler: A golf ball with a smile. A popular choice for a waterball. (See AMF *ball*, *waterball*.)

smoker: A hard, air-piercing, long-flying straight golf shot that leaves a contrail in its path.

smoke the ball (to): To hit a hard, air-piercing, long-flying, straight golf shot. As in: "Ben *smoked* a two-iron 220 yards down the fairway, but his ball ran into the foursome ahead and they threw his ball into the lake." (Also see *barbequing it, bomb.*)

smother it (to): To hit the ball with the club face hooded at impact, producing a low hooking trajectory. (See *quacker.*)

snail chaser: A term for a slow player. (See *mop squeezer, rescue operation, roadblock.*)

snail trail: A golf course prone to slow play. As in: "We flew through the first five holes, hoping to finish before dark, but then ran into a rescue operation and were back on the *snail trail.*

snake: A very long putt that slithers around multiple breaks before going into the hole. (See *Putting Measurements* diagram, page 53.)

snake bit: Someone who suffers a streak of bad luck, as in: "Greg Norman was *snake bit* on 14 and ended up losing the tournament."

snake charmer: A golfer who makes a lot of snakes.

SMOKING THE BALL

snake kisser: A very low shot. (See *Low Trajectory Shots* diagram, page 92.)

snap-hook: An extremely annoying tee shot where the ball veers off immediately to the left after impact and disappears into the woods or in a water hazard. (See *duck hook, EMBO, quacker*.)

sniper: A slightly less severe version of the snap hook. The ball may end up in the spinach instead of the woods.

snowman: A score of 8. For example: "Mrs. O'Connor was on the green in three, but her putter turned suddenly cold and she ran head into the old snowman." (See *dog balls, Frosty*.)

snuggles: Coy way of saying your approach shot finished next to the pin. Annoying. (See *birdie territory, dead, makeable, stake*.)

softy: A balata ball in pro talk.

solid: Adjective or adverb used to describe a smooth and powerful connection between the ball and the club head. For example: "I hit the ball *solid*, but it struck a branch and was never to be seen again."

A SOLITAIRE

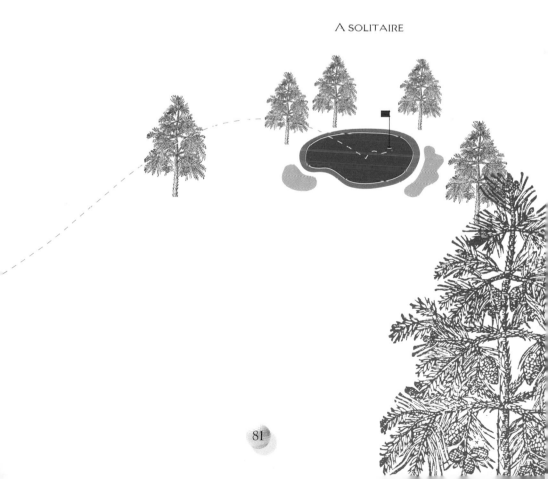

Solitaire: An exquisite hole in one. Also known as an ace.

South America: A putt needing one more revolution. Also known as a Central America. (See *The World of Golf* diagram, page 35.)

southpaw: Golfer who needs to read instruction books upside down.

spade: A six-iron.

spade-mashie: Extinct species of wrench similar to the modern six-iron.

spaghetti: A high, tangly type of rough.

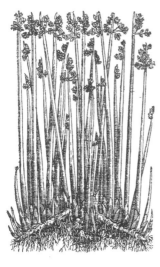

SPAGHETTI

spatula: A 60-degree wedge. (See *flop shot, pancake, skull.*)

spikes: Slang for golf shoes. (See *cleats.*)

spinach: Thick rough.

spit it out: Words of command addressed at the peaceful sylvan surroundings after they have swallowed your golf ball.

splashie: A par made after hitting from a watery lie.

split the fairway: To hit a straight drive right over the middle of the fairway. As in: "Joe's drive looked like it was gonna *split the fairway* at first, but suddenly it started leaking to the right, then the wind took it and the ball was gonzo."

spoon: Old-fashioned name for the three-wood.

spray: To hit shots in random directions. (Also see *aerosol man.*)

squib: A semi-skulled ball that bounces along the fairway. Borrowed from football.

stake: Same as flagstick, flagpole, and pin. To stake it requires the golfer to hit the ball within two or three feet of the hole, without any roll. For example: "From where we stood it looked like Dave had staked it, but when we reached the green we were happy to find that his ball had rolled into the back bunker."

stick: 1) A term for a golf club. For example: "The airline lost my bag and, playing with my wife's *sticks*, I shot the best round of my life." or 2) Short for flagstick. As in: "My 60-foot putt went straight for the *stick*, and would have gone in if I'd only given it a little more gas." (Also see *cozy it up*, *dead*, *pin*, *snuggles*, *stiff*.)

stiff: An approach shot that ends up very close to the hole. For example: "George's shot from the rough was *stiff* at the pin, and he was just about to tap it in when he noticed that he had played the wrong ball."

stoggie soaker: An enthusiastic shot hit from a water hazard while smoking a cigar.

stony: A ball that lands like a stone at the hole. (Also see *dead*, *snuggles*, *stiff*.)

stretcher-bearer: Another term for a caddy. (Also see *bag rat*, *bird dog*, *looper*.)

stripe (to): To hit a powerful tee shot.

striper: A range ball. For example: "Alfred sliced his tee shot towards the driving range, and his brand new balata ball was lost among the *stripers*."

strip mining: To take large divots.

stub: A putt hit fat.

stymie: A golf word of important historical significance whose definition can be found in serious golf dictionaries.

Sun Tan City: Popular golfing mecca in Saudi Arabia. (See *The World of Golf* diagram, page 35.)

Sunset Strip: A score of 77, referring to a popular American television show of the 1950s. More likely to be heard on the Senior tour these days.

sweater-and-shoe pro: Derogatory name used by touring professionals to designate club professionals.

swing doctor: A teaching professional.

swing oil: The liquid refreshment that lubricates the swing. Dispensed without a prescription at the emergency room. Also known as aiming fluid.

swipe: A full-blown swing with somewhat of an unorthodox style. As in: "Ben took a *swipe* at it, but all he could do was bury the ball deeper in the sand."

TAP-IN

tap-in: A putt measured in inches rather than feet. Usually considered a gimme, unless you are playing for serious candy.

Tarzan: A player who enjoys hanging around the jungle.

Taxi!: An expression used to tease an opponent when his or her ball cruises by the hole. For example: "It was the seventh time Bernie had yelled *Taxi!* since the beginning of the round and Fred finally punched him in the face."

T.C. Chen: The art of striking the ball two times in one shot, made famous in 1985 by T.C. Chen at the U.S. Open. Sometimes referred to as a double Chen.

teaser: A delicate short putt.

tempura: Japanese equivalent of a pop-up shot

tentative prod: A weak putt that stops short of the hole. (Also see *girlish*.)

tester: A short but difficult shot under pressure.

Texas wedge: The putter, when used someplace other than the green. As in: "At the 18th, Mrs. Breggenburger wisely opted for the *Texas wedge* from the fringe, but the pressure was too much and she stubbed it anyway."

that dog will hunt: An expression with the same meaning as that'll play, only more colorful and endearing, especially to hunters and dog lovers.

A Toe Job from the Tips

GOLF ARCHETYPES

THE VAST MAJORITY OF GOLFERS FALL INTO ONE OF THE FOLLOWING CATEGORIES:

- AEROSOL MAN
- AUDITOR
- BAG RAT
- BALL HAWKER
- BANKER
- BARBER
- BIRDIE BOY/GIRL
- BOSS OF THE MOSS
- BUCKSHOT BILLY
- CABBAGE POUNDER
- CHEERLEADER
- DEW SWEEPER
- DIMPLEHEAD
- DOUBLE LOOPER
- DUB
- DUFFER
- GOLF LAWYER
- GOLF WIDOW
- HACKER
- JAMALIE
- JUNK MAN
- KEG MAN
- LAW DOG
- MOP SQUEEZER
- NATURE BOY/GIRL
- PIGEON
- PIZZA CHEF
- POOL SHARK
- PLUMBER
- ROODLE
- SNAIL CHASER
- SWEATER AND SHOE PRO
- TRUNK SLAMMER
- TURF SPANKER
- WALLBANGER

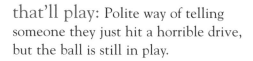

that'll play: Polite way of telling someone they just hit a horrible drive, but the ball is still in play.

thin: A shot where the ball is caught with the bottom part of the clubface and travels on a lower trajectory than normal. Generally speaking, thin is better than fat.

throw-up zone: The area immediately surrounding the hole. Depending on how strong your stomach is, the *throw-up zone* ranges from one to six feet around the cup. (See *Putting Measurement* diagram, page 53.)

thunder stick: The driver. (Also see *big dog, chief, lumber*.)

tiddler: A short putt.

tiger country: Thick, wooded rough. Not to be confused with Tiger Woods. (See *jungle, mahoofka*.)

Tiger cubs: Young Tiger Woods followers and emulators.

Tigermania: Psychological mass phenomenon requiring non-stop Tiger Woods media coverage even if someone else is actually winning.

tiger tees: The back tees. They were called the *tiger tees* even before Tiger Woods. Really.

Timber!: Another annoying expression used when someone's ball is headed hard for the woods. As in: "If Bernie hadn't already left the course with a broken nose, he probably would have yelled *timber!* when Nick's ball disappeared into the woods."

tin: Slang for the golf hole. Holes were once lined with tin. (Also see *barrel, can, cup, jar*.)

tin cup: An impossible, foolish shot. As in: "Omigod! Van de Velde just pulled a *tin cup* on the 18th at Carnoustie!"

tips: The farthest back-tee markers on a golf course. As in: "At 120 bucks a round, might as well get our money's worth and play from the *tips.*" (Also see *blues, tiger tees.*)

tivot: A divot taken while hitting on the tee.

touch: Ability to make delicate chips and putts.

toe jam: Tasty expression for a toe job.

toe job: Hitting the ball with the toe end of the club face. Disastrous with a wood.

toilet flusher: A putt that swirls around the rim of the hole before draining.

TOILET FLUSHER

tool box: The golf bag. (Also see *quiver, sack.*)

top (to): To make contact with the top of the ball. (Also see *skull.*)

top shelf: The upper plateau on a two-tier green.

toupee: A thin divot. (See *The Dirt on Divots* diagram, page 32.)

tour swing: An upright swing, learned while on the university golf team

tracer ammo: Day-Glo balls used for night golf.

track: A type of golf course. A golf course is generally beautiful, challenging. A *track* is arduous, demanding, tough. (See *dog track.*)

transcontinental: Similar to an ocean liner, a term for a very long putt.

trap: Short for sandtrap. (Also see *beach, catbox.*)

tree iron: An iron shot that ends up in the lumberyard. Also refers to the club used to perpetrate the shot.

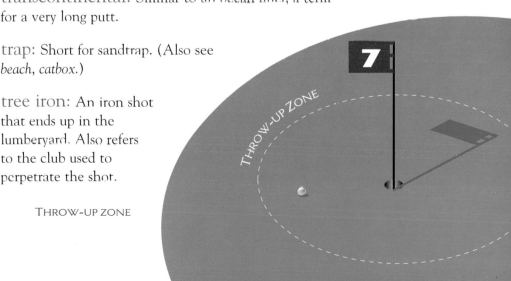

THROW-UP ZONE

trench wrench: The sand wedge.

triple: Short for triple bogey or three shots above par on a hole. The ugly but inescapable reality of life as an average golfer.

trombones: A score of 76.

truck: The golf cart. (Also see *BIPmobile, hummer.*)

trunk-slammer: Originally a term to describe golf pros who didn't make the cut at a tournament. Sometimes used to describe a golfer who uses his car as a locker room. By extension, a municipal or public course golfer.

turf spanker: A really bad golfer, as one may infer from the term. Sometimes the spankers ought to be the spankees. The Marquis de Sod was a turf spanker.

turn: The transition between the front and the back nine. Notice how golf offers the opportunity for redemption, or a royal opportunity to screw up after a good first half.

TURF SPANKER

tv shot: A professional-looking shot, similar to a career shot.

tweeter: Cute word for birdie. People who say tweeter also say snuggles.

two-holer: A double green. A crass way to describe one of modern golf architects' treasured re-discoveries.

two-shooter: A par-four if your handicap is low enough to talk that way.

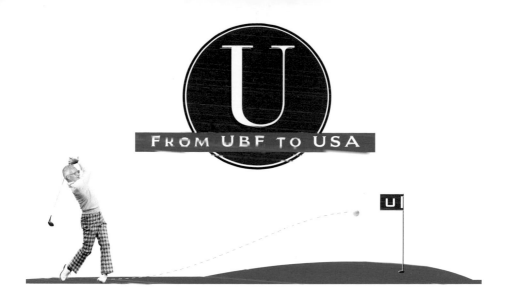

UBE: Acronym for Ugly But Effective.

under-clubbing: Hitting with a club that is too short to deliver the necessary distance.

up: In match play, to be up is to be in the lead by a certain number of holes. As in: "Davis was *two-up* at the turn, but he was feeling down as he had been *four-up* at the 5th."

up and down: The admirable or lucky act of getting the ball onto the green and into the hole in just two strokes. For example: "Paul needed a perfect sand shot to get *up and down* and save par, but instead he skulled the shot and his ball ended up down in the ravine."

USA: Acronym for the three most fateful words on the green: U Still Away.

USA

ACRONYMS OF GOLF

IN THIS BUSY WORLD, IT IS OFTEN CONVENIENT TO EMPLOY THE OCCASIONAL ACRONYM TO REPRESENT A COMMONLY USED PHRASE OR CONCEPT.

- ABSU
- ABFU
- AMF
- BIP
- BIPSIC
- DAP
- DSP
- EMBO
- FISA
- NITBY
- NITWY
- PBS
- ROB
- UBE
- USA
- USGA

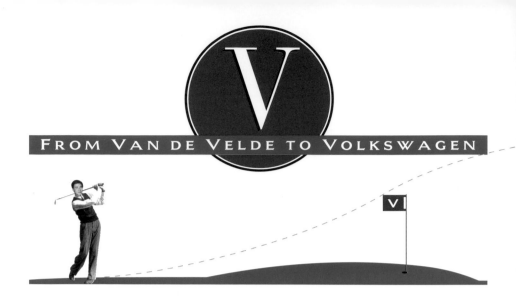

Van de Velde: Committing a terrible blunder on the last hole when the match is almost won. (See *tin cup*.)

Vin Skully: Another low-flying celebrity shot, i.e., a skulled shot.

virgin green: When no one in a group is able to hit the green on a par-3 hole, it is said to be a *virgin green*.

visor hair: Similar to hat hair but more pronounced. Fred Couples is particularly prone to *visor hair*.

volcano: Golf hole cut on top of a mound. (See *Marquis de Sod*.)

Volkswagen: A shot which makes up in efficiency what it lacks in style.

VIN SKULLY

wagon: Golf cart. As in: "I got off the *wagon*, picked up my three-wood and got back on the bogey train."

walk and whack: A degenerate version of The Royal and Ancient game.

wall banger: The fellow in cut-off jeans and a see-through t-shirt next to you at the driving range with a toe-jam problem.

water ball: A cheap, worn-out ball used exclusively to play over water hazards. *Water balls* tend to be resilient and will often last several rounds, while a brand new Titleist is doomed as soon as it's out of the sleeve. (See AMF *ball, smiler.*)

water wedge: The telescopic rod used to resurrect golf balls from their watery grave.

watery grave: The final resting place of many golf balls. Famous watery graves: The ponds in front of Augusta's 12th and 15th greens, and the lake surrounding the TPC at Sawgrass's 17th.

weapons of mass destruction: Term for golf clubs. More frequently used at the beginning of a round when the adrenaline is running.

whack: To strike the ball without any pretense of style or proper technique. (See *hacker.*)

wheels: What eventually comes off when a round is proceeding too well. As in: "Larry was cruising along the course shooting pars and bogeys, but the *wheels* finally came off on 13 after he drove into the hot-dog shed and carded a beagle."

whiff: An embarrassing shot in which the club head passes over the ball, never making contact. When playing with the boss, *whiffs* don't count. (Also see *airball, blow dry, drive-by shooting.*)

whippy: A golf club shaft with above-average flexibility. The adjective is quasi-derogatory when used by macho types. As in: "Darryl likes his new irons, but finds the shafts a little too *whippy* for his taste."

whitee: Old-fashioned, potentially offensive slang word for the golf ball. (Also see *pill.*)

whopper: A meaty, juicy, flame-broiled drive. (Also see *barbecuing it, smoking.*)

widow (golf): A fanatic golfer's spouse or significant other if he/she is not a golfer him/herself. Playing with your spouse or companion may offer relief but there are problems associated with that too. (See *divorce court.*)

Willie ball: A ball that lands on an adjacent road or on a cart path. Derived from famed country-music star Willie Nelson's song, *On the Road Again.* (Also see *cart-path management, Mario Andretti.*)

wind-cheater: A low-trajectory shot designed to keep the ball under the wind. Real, intentional *wind-cheaters* are rare. Most *wind-cheaters* are thin, semi-skulled shots.

wobbler: A type of putt that hops left and right of its intended line.

woodie: A par made after reaching the green with a wood. As in: "Joe was so excited about his new three-wood, he got a woodie on the first hole."

woodpecker: A ball flying into the woods and bouncing off the tree trunks with the unmistakable signature sound of the pileated *woodpecker*. (See *Spit it out*.)

working man's four: A term denoting a long, difficult par-4

worm-burner: The granddaddy of funny golf words. A shot that flies so low even dirt-loving invertebrates are not safe from its ravages. (See *Low Trajectory Shots*.)

wrenches: Another word for golf clubs. (Also see *sticks*.)

wristy: A swing style relying on the wrists to generate power. You can generally bet some decent money against a *wristy* golfer. (See *wheels, zip code*.)

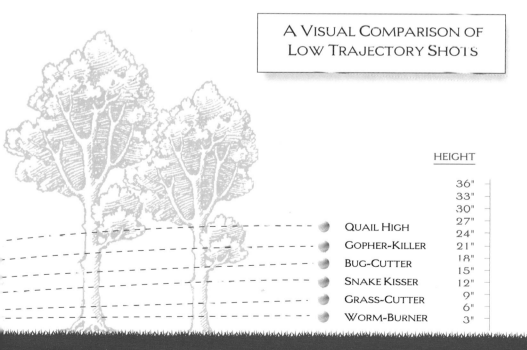

A VISUAL COMPARISON OF LOW TRAJECTORY SHOTS

HEIGHT

Shot	Height
	36"
	33"
	30"
	27"
QUAIL HIGH	24"
GOPHER-KILLER	21"
	18"
BUG-CUTTER	15"
SNAKE KISSER	12"
GRASS-CUTTER	9"
	6"
WORM-BURNER	3"

LADIES' TEE ⟶

yank: A bad golf swing resulting in the ball flying way left of its target. (Right for lefthanders.) As in "I skulled my first one in the drink, then *yanked* my second out of bounds. Good thing I had two Mulligans left!"

yard sale: Bags and clubs spilling over from the cart. As in: "Just after yanking his tee shot into the water, Chuck found himself in the middle of a *yard sale*."

Yasir Arafat: A shot that is rather unattractive and sitting in the sand.

yips: Psycho-physiological putting disorder afflicting middle-aged Tour players. The mysterious ailment generally cures itself just in time for the Senior tour.

Yogi the Bear. Affectionate name for the course ranger. (Also see *law dog*, *Marshall Dillon*.)

you da man: 1990s phrase used by tournament fans to express admiration for their golf heroes. Can be heard irrespective of the shot, especially on Sunday afternoon after the brewskis have kicked in.

You da man!

Z golf: Desirable form of golf for those in need of exercise. The shots are alternating left to right until reaching the hole. (Also see *army golf, military golf, Zorro.*)

zap: To hit a quick, firm putting stroke. A first cousin of rap. To *zap* it past the hole indicates the missile has missed its target.

zeppelin: A high, floating shot soon to crash and burn. (See *Ascending Tee Shots* diagram, page 40.)

zip code (next): An area on or off the golf course, well to the right or left of the fairway you're aiming for.

Zorro: An entire hole played from left rough to right rough without ever touching the fairway. Mask optional.

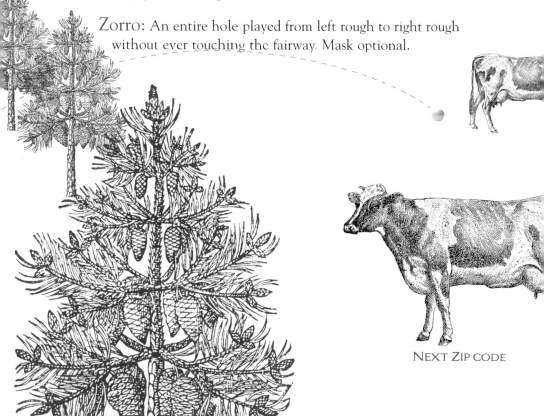

NEXT ZIP CODE

Welcome Enterprises, Inc.
588 Broadway
New York, New York 10012

HarperCollins books may be purchased for educational,
business, or sales promotional use. For information, please write
to: Special Markets Department, HarperCollins Publishers, Inc.,
10 East 53rd Street, New York, New York 10022.

Library of Congress Cataloging-in-Publication Data

Tiegreen, Mary.
  Let the big dog eat: a dictionary of golf's colorful
vernacular/by Mary Tiegreen and Hubert Pedroli
     p.cm.
  ISBN 0-688-17576-7
  1. Golf—Terminology. 2. Pedroli, Hubert.
II. Title.
GV961.3. T54 2000
796.352'01'4—dc21   99-058054

Printed in China

First Edition

1 2 3 4 5 6 7 8 9 10

www.harpercollins.com